Sissy Jones
Cell— 901-212-8917

Kings &
Queens
of
England and Scotland

David Piper

Kings & Queens

of England and Scotland

Frederick Muller Limited
London

Frontispiece: Victoria and Albert with dead game
(detail), by Sir Edwin Landseer, c. 1842. Oil on
canvas, $44\frac{1}{2} \times 56\frac{1}{2}$ in (113×143.5 cm). Royal
Collection

The illustrations on the cover are:

Front, left: Henry VIII by Hans Holbein the Younger.
Oil and tempera on panel, $11 \times 7\frac{1}{2}$ in (28×19 cm).
Lugano, Thyssen-Bornemisza Collection
Front, right: Her Majesty Queen Elizabeth II
by Pietro Annigoni (Plate 158)
Back, above: Edward VI as a child by Holbein
(Plate 83)
Back, below: Queen Victoria (detail), by Thomas
Sully (Plate 135)

This revised edition first published in Great Britain in
1984 by Frederick Muller Limited, Dataday House,
Alexandra Road, London, SW19 7JZ
First edition published 1980

ISBN 0 584 11085 5

Printed in Italy by Istituto d'Arti Grafiche, Bergamo

CONTENTS

1. Edward IV in council. c. 1470–1. British Library,
Royal Ms 15E iv, f.14

6

INTRODUCTION

Thackeray, visiting Paris in the late 1830s, observed one of the most famous, successful and widely imitated of all royal portraits, Hyacinthe Rigaud's painting of Louis XIV in 1701. In a drawing Thackeray analysed the recipe. To one shrivelled, meagre, bald old man, thin-shanked, stick-leaning, add: a froth of ermine, gold fleurs-de-lys, lace and curling wig: plump up the legs till they strut, and transpose the stick into a golden sceptre. Serve as the Sun King himself, the cynosure of all Europe.

The analysis is not all that unjust, but is unkind, and takes no account either of the fact that, as long as royalty exists, royal portraits are a political necessity, or of the superb quality of Rigaud's response to one of the most difficult problems that can confront any portraitist. The basic reason for the fascination of the royal portrait, the portrait of the head of state, is that in it you can see most vividly the conflict which emerges sooner or later in all forms of portraiture – between the ideal and the factual, the general and the particular. The royal painter has to reflect the enduring and majestic nature of the office, while simultaneously fusing into the image the individual, unique and recognizable likeness of the mortal inhabitant of that office.

In practice, of course, the portraitist's solutions swing from one extreme to the other; the royal portrait can be really little more than a likeness of the throne, crown, sceptre and orb – as in the Great Seals up to Henry VIII's – or it can be, as any other portrait, essentially an attempt to capture the likeness of an individual human being,

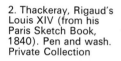

2. Thackeray, Rigaud's Louis XIV (from his Paris Sketch Book, 1840). Pen and wash. Private Collection

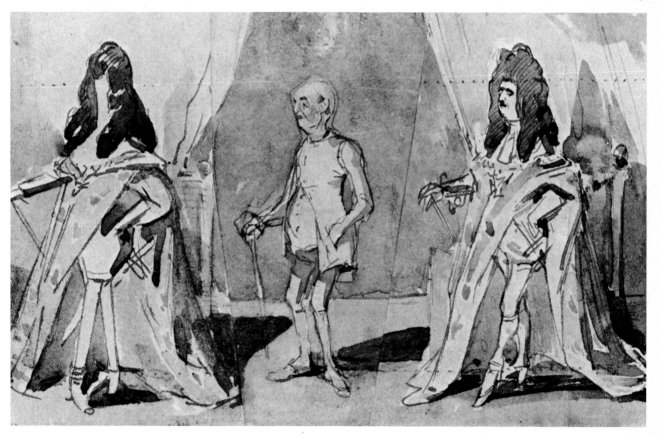

naked at some point in his lonely journey from the dark into the light of life and out again into the dark of death. The latter kind of solution only occurs when interest in individuality, that quality in a man which makes him different from anyone else, has become a reigning obsession: that is, in terms of European culture, in Greek and Roman times or after the Renaissance. In the long gap between these two periods, artists' interest in exploring an individual likeness dwindled and indeed all but vanished for several centuries. Early Christian emphasis was not on man on earth, but on what he would become in the life hereafter: man is the servant of God, and it is either in this guise or as virtually pure symbols that the earliest kings in Britain, their personalities cohering obscurely through the mists of what were once called the Dark Ages, are glimpsed. The medium in which they first manifest themselves is the coinage, and then, even more generalized, in the seals.

The first English – or more accurately, Anglo-Saxon – king to have an image representing him reproduced in the coinage was a very obscure king of Mercia, called Peada, in the mid-seventh century AD. Any personal individuality in this is, however, minimal, for the image is borrowed almost verbatim from a widely circulated coin of Constantine the Great. It is, nevertheless, the first instance of the profile of authority appearing on coins in Britain. Late in the following century there appears a silver penny of Offa, King of the Mercians (757-96) (Plate 26), that has been claimed as one of the earliest attempts at a real likeness of a British king – a pop-eyed profile indicating something of a unique personality perhaps, but much more securely identified by his name, printed loud and clear. In essentials, in fact, his image follows the Constantine pattern: he wears a diadem (not a crown) and the profile is clean-shaven. Anglo-Saxon kings, then and for more than two hundred years on, were probably bearded, yet almost always shown clean-shaven on their coins.

A century later the king whose name would occur probably to most non-historians as being the earliest king of England, even if only owing to the potency of the whiff of (doubtless mythical) burnt cakes lingering on the air through a millennium – Alfred, King of Wessex (871-99) – seems on his coinage (Plate 27) to have become even less, rather than more, distinct as an individual, and to be in even graver need of his name alongside (although on some rare coins his image is shown bearded). Alfred is still diademed – which may reflect the importance at the time in the ceremony of royal investiture of the anointing rather than of the crowning.

Æthelstan, King of Wessex (924-39), seems to be the first to be shown with a crown on his coins, and he was the first king of all England. Later Æthelraed, famously 'the Unready' (978-1016), elaborated the supporting regalia, showing on some coins the royal sceptre. With Edward the Confessor, accustomed from his long exile on the Continent to rather more sophisticated styles, the king's image developed in some variety on different coins. A hint of realism appears in a bearded version, and then – a radical innovation for England – he appears enthroned, crowned, with sceptre and orb. He appears just so on his Great Seal (Plates 33, 34), as we shall see, and in a late type of coin his crown, until then a conventional English circlet with flowered points, gives way to an imperial-type crown with arches, as found on the Continent, while in a variant of an even later type of coin he appears full-face wearing a fashionable Saxon moustache. Generalized though such likenesses were, they reflect the classical practice of stamping authority on the coinage in the form of the profile, or less often the frontal face, of the head of state. The head here is established as the standard symbol of validity, and so on our coins today it still is.

Up to the eleventh century coins were the only medium through which an image of the ruler could become common knowledge. From then on, however, an alternative vehicle is found in many surviving seals. The practice of validating documents by attaching to them wax impressions from a seal is of great antiquity. When kings were illiterate, the seal authorized the document, as a signature was to do later. The die, or matrix, from which impressions were taken was, of course, very precious, and its security and its use jealously guarded: just as a signature, it could authorize almost anything and, fallen into wrong hands, could be used for very dangerous ends. The wax impression was usually attached to its document by a dangling ribbon or thong, so that it had two sides, each of which could carry an image. The images to begin with were still more generalized than those on coins and, of course, much rarer, although a seal could, like a coin, be duplicated more or less indefinitely, being a wax impression taken from a mould.

As on coins, the images on seals were symbols of authority. They were, and are, also symbols of fascinating stamina: on one side is the figure that art historians call the 'majesty figure', in which form those invested with supreme power, from God downwards, have been shown through the ages. This is a whole-length figure, forthrightly

3. Henry VIII's third Great Seal, c. 1542 (enlarged). British Museum

INTRODUCTION

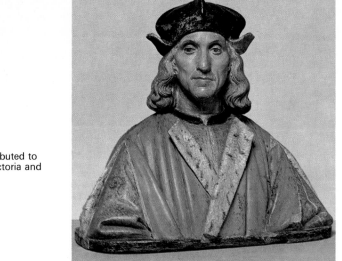

4. Polychrome bust of Henry VII attributed to Torrigiano; probably posthumous. Victoria and Albert Museum

frontal, seated on the throne with crown, sceptre and orb – image of the final judge and arbiter. On the other side of the seal is an armed figure on horseback – the conqueror, the defender and so on. These two images have persisted from at least William the Conqueror in the eleventh century to Elizabeth II in the twentieth. The only break came during the Commonwealth, when various alternatives were tried (including a representation, within a circle three or four inches across, of the whole House of Commons in session – it having replaced the executed Charles I as the ultimate arbiter and judge). The figures on the Great Seal long remained pure symbol, the same design on occasions serving two or more kings in succession, with only the name being altered. The design became more elaborate and in Henry II's time was modulated in an attempt at classical elegance, but it is only in the reign of Henry VIII that in his third Great Seal (Plate 3) the flesh-and-blood individuality of Henry Tudor bursts through the prim royal puppet in its spiky Gothic niche that had sufficed on his first two seals. There are few more vivid illustrations in English art of the impact of Renaissance humanism, but the essential symbols that they depict remain unaltered, and are still so now four and a half centuries later.

In pictorial or full sculptural terms the earliest survivors of royal portraiture came in the form of illuminations in manuscripts and then of tomb effigies. Representations

5. Henry VIII. The handsomeness of his youth is hinted at by L. Horenbout's miniature of him of about 1526. Fitzwilliam Museum, Cambridge

6. Edward VI. This image, by Holbein's successor, William Scrots, was disseminated in numerous versions and clearly reflects Holbein's image of Henry VIII. c. 1550. Panel, 66 × 36 in (168 × 91 cm). Royal Collection

of kings can be found in manuscripts as early as the tenth century, but although kingship is indicated by a crown and the fashion of the times by their beards, they appear, unlike on the coins, as supporting figures in the service of religion: Æthelstan presenting Bede's *Life of St Cuthbert* to the saint (Plate 28); Eadgar (the Pacific; reigned 959-75), in 966 adoring saints, angels, and Christ in a mandorla (Plate 30); Cnut (reigned 1016-35) and his queen Ælfgyfu presenting a cross to the new minster at Winchester. Cnut is – and needs to be – identified by his name, as too is William the Conqueror on the Bayeux Tapestry, that unique record. The Norman designer of the tapestry does, however, make an apparently consistent, if elementary, differentiation between the two sides: Normans are clean-shaven, the Anglo-Saxons moustached (Plates 36 and 39).

Sculptured effigies began a century or so later in the strange shrine of English kings in the abbey church of Fontevrault near the Loire (Plates 44, 46 and 47). With Henry II (d. 1189) and Richard Coeur-de-Lion (d. 1199) are Henry's queen Eleanor of Aquitaine, and Isabella, queen of Richard's brother and successor King John. They are shown as dead on ceremonial biers or beds, the kings crowned and robed, the sceptres resting on their breasts, the swords discarded at their side: so accoutred, they would have been carried to burial. As likenesses, however, they are retrospective and obviously generalized as to facial character, although two very different men are obviously represented. Thereafter, for perhaps three hundred years, the most vivid record of kings survives on their tombs, although the record is incomplete and until Richard II highly uncertain as evidence of faithful likenesses. But vivid some of them certainly are. John's effigy lies not at Fontevrault but at Worcester – crowned, open-eyed in death, broad and flat-cheeked, yet vulpine; but it is not a portrait, the features, striking though they are, being more or less a stock-in-trade of the sculptors of the Purbeck School who made this after the king's death (Plate 48). The same is true of the Black Prince: his effigy at Canterbury (Plate 56) – helmeted, the staring face framed by the chain-mail bib over which the symmetrical moustaches droop – is impressive, yet is a sculptor's convention. Its virtual twin is the effigy of Sir Thomas Beauchamp at Warwick. The noblest of all is perhaps the very idealized, almost Christ-like, interpretation of the murdered Edward II at Gloucester (Plate 53).

Most impressive, however, is the great sequence of royal tombs that gird the shrine of the Confessor and the seat of majesty, the coronation chair, in Westminster Abbey. Of them Francis Beaumont wrote: 'Here are sands, ignoble things, Dropt from the ruin'd sides of Kings . . .'. Those of Henry III and his daughter-in-law Eleanor of Castile were commissioned in 1291 by Edward I from the London goldsmith William Torel (Plates 49 and 52). Edward III's (d. 1377) effigy (Plate 55), in which a strong element of likeness is probably introduced, as beautifully and austerely stylized as it is, seems essentially to depend for the head on that (still surviving at the Abbey) of the wooden funeral effigy carried at his funeral and based on a deathmask. Then there are the tombs of Richard II and his queen Anne of Bohemia – serene effigies commissioned by Richard himself after the death of his wife with the specification in the contract that the images should 'conterfait' (i.e. resemble) their subjects (Plate 59). Here likeness does indeed enter in, for that of Richard is the first that can be checked adequately against other extant and authentic likenesses: that in the famous Wilton

Diptych (Plate 58), a beautiful example of the International Gothic style of the finest quality, in the National Gallery in London, and that in the colossal majesty-figure painting of Richard that still hangs in Westminster Abbey (Plate 57). All three representations, although quite independent, agree on the characteristics of Richard's physiognomy.

Thereafter, as in the case of the seals, the convention of tomb-portraiture in royal effigies is established, but the subsequent gaps are very pronounced. With Henry VII's great bronze tomb in his chapel at Westminster, modelled by Michelangelo's rival Torrigiano, the convention is altered by the High Renaissance style, but the symbolism remains constant. Although Edward VI and Mary I are missing, Elizabeth I and Mary Queen of Scots lie close by, their effigies set in northern Mannerist variations of the theme. Then, however, the tradition fell into abeyance, and the statues by which subsequent monarchs are remembered are rather the equestrian ones, from Le Sueur's Charles I situated at the top of Whitehall through even to that charming rarity, Wyatt's George III at the end of Pall Mall (Plate 122), in which one of the most pompous conventions of royal portraiture is actually imbued with modesty. Only in Victoria's reign, in the newly established royal mausoleum at Frogmore and not at Westminster, was the royal tomb effigy enthusiastically revived.

Then, clearly closely related to the tomb effigies, there are the funeral effigies. They are, in fact, a preliminary phase in the evolution of effigies, made for the actual funeral, preceded by a lying or standing in state, and considered as ephemeral. They seem always to have been likenesses. In a lying in state they represented (and perhaps replaced) the body itself, bearing witness that the body's inhabitant, and no other, was dead, and opening the way for the legitimate successor. Vivid survivors of the funeral effigies form the 'Ragged Regiment' in the museum at Westminster Abbey, from the fourteenth to the early eighteenth century. The heads of some of them, in a disturbing waxy brilliance, offer most convincing portraits of their sitters – Charles II, like a cynical ageing Hollywood film-star, is entirely satisfactory and credible. And it was in this form that Oliver Cromwell posthumously achieved the royal status that he never accepted in life (Plate 100). Crowned, sceptred and robed in ermine, his effigy stood in state, after his death in 1658, in Somerset House. After the Restoration the effigy was hung by the neck from a window, but what may well be its head, naked of a wig and with bulging glass eyes, survives unexpectedly in the Bargello in Florence.

The earliest easel paintings, as far as originals are concerned, are those of Henry VII. They start in small scale, quite modest head-and-shoulders in the Van Eyckian tradition, and they certainly were likenesses. Retrospective sets of them became fashionable in the sixteenth century, the earlier ones, going back even to Edward the Confessor, being purely fictitious likenesses, although some of the later ones from Richard II onwards may reflect now lost originals taken from life. It is in this form that the kings of Scotland first emerge from faceless anonymity into the light. A set of sixteenth-century paintings of Stewart kings, starting with James I (reigned 1406–37) and closing with James V (d. 1542), is in the Scottish Portrait Gallery, and they all may record authentic traditions of likeness (Plates 16, 17, 20). But of James III and James V there are other, more spectacular, witnesses; James III in the superbly grave wings of

7. Charles I on horseback, by Van Dyck, a copy of a picture painted for St James's Palace and now in the Royal Collection. Corsham Court, Wiltshire

a diptych by Hugo van der Goes (Plate 18), and also commemorated in a silver groat of about 1485, claimed as the 'earliest Renaissance coin portrait outside Italy' – a cogent reminder that Scotland's ties with Continental fashions could be more up-to-date than that of the Tudor court in London. So too Mary Queen of Scots (and before that, wife to the heir to the throne of France) in her tragic, but international, career, sat to Clouet in France and to Hilliard in England, the finest artists of their time in the north (Plates 24 and 25). Her tomb was erected at Westminster by her son James VI of Scotland and I of England in whom the two countries were united.

In the transcontinental marriage negotiations of the sixteenth century, portraits travelled as proxies for wooer and wooed – that by Michiel Sittow of Henry VII (Plate 70) went for inspection by daughters of Maximilian (apparently unsuccessfully). As the art of the naturalistic portrait quickly established itself, it answered other proxy duties; thus, for example, a royal portrait became a standard item in an ambassador's baggage, lending authority to him in his residence abroad, as even now in embassies and consulates everywhere the visitor is confronted by a copy or reproduction of the state portrait, or even a photograph, of the Queen. Owners of large houses used to have long loyal sequences of paintings of the kings and queens of England. All this inevitably meant considerable reduplication and, in relation to the considerable number of paintings of any monarch surviving, only a handful will be 'originals'. They tend generally to the formal. While early on there may have been some attempt to hold a monopoly on certain sizes, such as the whole-length life-scale portrait, as very suitable only for very important persons, this obviously could not last and by the early seventeenth century whole-lengths were commonplace.

8. Statuette of George III by F. Hardenberg. 1820. 11 in (29 cm) high. National Portrait Gallery

The royalty of the sitter, therefore, still generally needed 'labelling' by the introduction of the attributes of royalty – crowns, ermine, robes, orb, sceptre and so on. This can lead to accusations of insincerity, such as those indicated in Thackeray's dissection of Rigaud's Louis XIV; on the other hand, a painter of genius could transcend the formula, the most notable examples being Holbein and Van Dyck. Their recordings, so convincing as to seem definitive, have profoundly influenced posterity's assessment of Henry VIII and Charles I.

Holbein, in his projection of a formidable physical personality (Plate 76), manages to project also the sensation of majesty – or, at least, of ruthless supreme power – without more usual attributes of kingship: no crown, sceptre and orb, no coronation robes, although the costume is splendid and the setting richly elaborate. It is not a comfortable image, but it convinces, and it is surely Holbein's image that Sir Walter Raleigh about 1614 had in mind when he wrote in his *History of the World:* 'for King Henry the Eighth, if all the Pictures and Patterns of a merciless Prince were lost in the World, might all again be painted to the Life, out of the Story of this King.'

Van Dyck, who in his portraits formulated the ideal image for the English gentleman and aristocrat to mirror himself on (not always successfully), painted Charles I in many guises. But he conveyed in all of them an easy, if melancholic, dignity, with romantic overtures of doom reflected in the story that when Bernini was confronted by the triple portrait by Van Dyck (Plate 95), from which he was to carve a bust of the king, the Italian sculptor was moved to tears. Van Dyck died in 1641 even before the beginning of the Civil Wars that were to culminate in the beheading of the king on the scaffold outside his Banqueting House in Whitehall in 1649; but to posterity Van Dyck seems to have recorded not only the true image (although other artists' views give very differing impressions), but to have painted Charles the Martyr before the event. An eighteenth-century painter, Northcote, admiring a version of one of Van Dyck's portraits of the king, exclaimed that it was a head fit to paint the Saviour from. Walter Scott in *Woodstock* has Cromwell standing thwarted before a portrait of the by then executed Charles I – 'That Flemish painter! that Antonio Vandyke – what a power he has! Steel may mutilate, warriors may waste and destroy – still the King stands, uninjured by time . . .'

But kings and queens, like other mortals, have families and friends, and it is for their pleasure that the more informal portraits are generally made. These are, however, proportionately very rare, and it is in formal guise that the faces of monarchs became known to ever-increasing numbers of their subjects by ever-increasingly sophisticated methods of reproduction. Mass reduplication by means of engravings was brought to a high pitch of excellence through the seventeenth and eighteenth centuries, although towards the end of that time scurrilous counterblasts in the form of libellous caricatures, penny-plain, twopence-coloured, became common, a symptom of the gradual abandonment of all claims to absolutism and divine right by constitutional monarchy.

Caricature, however, was by no means always aggressive or vicious. Even Gillray's evocation of George IV (when Prince of Wales) as a voluptuary suffering the horrors of

10. *Eliza Triumphans,* engraving by W. Rogers. This has the same theme as Gheeraert's painting (Plate 90), set out almost in geometric demonstration. 15 × 10 in (38 × 25 cm). British Museum

9. Mary Queen of Scots, lead medal by J. Primavera. c. 1572. British Museum

ELIZA, TRIVMPHANS

indigestion (Plate 15), if not exactly flattering, is very far from the savage distortion of his more typical work. Entirely credible as a realistic likeness of its subject, in mood almost of Dutch genre characterization, it betrays something perhaps of the latent affection, often unexpectedly mutual, that can link a cartoonist and his victim. The later silhouette of George IV (now trousered) with his brother the Duke of York (Plate 124) engagingly recalls Tweedledum and Tweedledee. Oil paintings of anywhere near such informality are not common. Jan van der Vaart's *Mary II* (Plate 111), seemingly almost acting as model for the literally high fashion of the *fontange* head-dressing of the 1690s, is a very early, but charming and humane, oddity. George III, a good family man (in intention and inclination anyway, if not very successfully *vis-à-vis* his obstreperous heir), employed the most accomplished master of the second wave of

conversation pieces, the German-born John Zoffany, to record royal domesticity. The result could be incongruous; there is one version of the royal family posed in full Van Dyck gear and attitudes – then very fashionable attributes supplied by many society portrait painters for their sitters – which, as an attempt to invest the staid, doubtless rather boring, image of the Georgian court with the cavalier glamour of the Caroline court, must be acknowledged as unconvincing. Zoffany's view of Queen Charlotte at her dressing-table, however (Plate 120), is one of the most charming of eighteenth-century small-scale portraits in an interior – the latter delineated with loving detailed accuracy.

In Victoria's reign the proliferation became enormous in all media – paintings, engravings, popular prints, statues, busts. Then came the postage stamp and, of course, the fundamental revolution, the photograph. Early photographs – needing a formal posing – could be to a considerable degree controlled in the interests of decorum and the desirability of royalty putting its best face forward, although they did tend, nevertheless, to reveal that clothes even on a queen might not fit as faultlessly as feathers on a bird.

At the other extreme – at least of apparent permanency – came the multiplication of full-scale (or larger) statues of Victoria Imperatrix, staking out vast areas of the globe as property of the Empire. Statues occur from Charles I onwards, increasing in answer to the classical taste of the eighteenth century, but only proliferating through the British Empire, as once they had in the Roman Empire, in Victorian days (Plate 13).

By the late twentieth century the statuary of the monarch has dwindled. The real oil portrait, in gilt frame, nonetheless persists, and in a studio in Regent's Park the state portrait is duplicated by the dozen, in all sizes and by several different techniques, for distribution to government offices at home and abroad, while the Queen in her patience sits again and again – in a room allocated for that purpose – to painters for 'one-off' originals for societies, charities, companies and institutions of many kinds of which she is the Patron. The official state portrait is in itself an institution of convenience but almost more of necessity; were the Queen to sit afresh whenever a portrait of her was needed, she would have no time for any other occupation. The chosen painter makes the 'master' version, and from this copies are turned out – normally not by the master himself. Kneller's studio used to do William IIIs a dozen at a time; Allan Ramsay, to whom production of the state portrait of George III was allotted (Plate 123), employed Reinagle as his assistant and hardly touched a brush himself again, his income assured by the Royal monopoly. In the twentieth century the official state portrait has been in difficulties, not least because the costume and traditional trappings of monarchy have become increasingly remote from everyday life – they do not consort with motor cars very happily, nor for that matter with trousers, rather than breeches, and, of course, not at all with short skirts. The official version of Queen Elizabeth II (by Sir James Gunn) in a stiff regalia-encrusted traditional pose was not popular and was in fact largely supplanted by versions of Annigoni's famous portrait (Plate 158).

As a work of art its eclectic and derivative elements are easily analysed – and were, by generally hostile art critics. The English countryside modulates backwards into a landscape of the Florentine fifteenth century with rather odd surrealist accents. The

13. Victoria, bust by E.O. Ford in the Mansion House, London

14. George IV's personal flamboyance is answered by Sir Thomas Lawrence's whole-length portrait, both one of the most spectacular and latest in the long tradition of state portraiture deriving from Van Dyck. Detail. Vatican, Rome

drawing may not be quite up to Leonardo's standards – the indication of the arm under the cloak, for example, is anatomically inadequate. But no quibbles can detract from the figure's essential and compelling simplicity; Elizabeth II is not presented as dummy festooned with crown, sceptre and ermine, but as a woman of flesh and blood and not in fancy dress. She may be wearing the Mantle of the Order of the Garter – and indeed she is, with its Star blazoned – but the garment is a most becoming midnight blue, and she has just picked it up and cast it casually about her shoulders against the nip in the air; it happened to be lying there to hand. And yet, of course, that is not quite true, and she is presented in part as fantasy figure but within a mythology, not of the obsolescent past, but of our own time. In the same year as this portrait was painted Grace Kelly had demonstrated, by marrying Prince Rainier of Monaco, that a film-star could become, not only on the screen, but in real life, royal – a princess. It was Annigoni's virtue to endow real majesty with the glamour of a film-star: a glamour instantly recognizable and valid throughout the world, out-Hollywooding Hollywood.

But even solutions such as Annigoni's are for formal and contrived occasions. In everyday life, whether formal or informal, royalty has become all too vulnerable to attack by the ubiquitous candid camera, as films get even faster and faster and zoom lenses peer into bedrooms from hundreds of yards away. The result can be enchanting – Charles Knight's capture of Queen Victoria's smile (Plate 136) – or embarrassing, impertinent and a disgusting invasion of human privacy, to which even royalty has a human right. And with television more and more of royalty's life – and possibly even death – becomes instant entertainment flickering in millions of homes: a power for endless good and perhaps equally endless danger.

A VOLUPTUARY under the horrors of Digestion.

15. By contrast, 'A Voluptuary under the Horrors of Digestion' is a caricature of George IV satirizing his habits. By James Gillray, 1792. 13 × 11 in (33 × 27 cm). National Portrait Gallery

THE HOUSE OF STEWART
IN SCOTLAND

IACOBVS·I·D·GRAT
REX·SCOTORVM

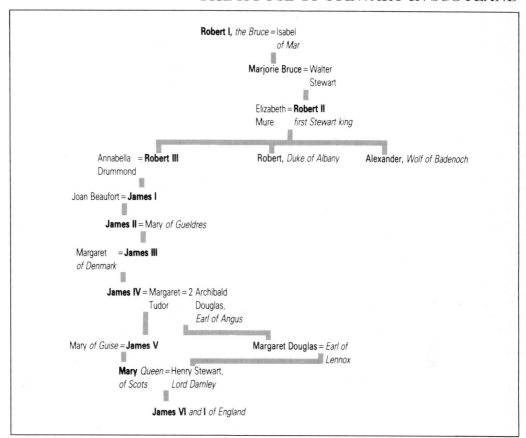

Robert I, *the Bruce* = Isabel *of Mar*

Marjorie Bruce = Walter Stewart

Elizabeth Mure = **Robert II** *first Stewart king*

Annabella Drummond = **Robert III**   Robert, *Duke of Albany*   Alexander, *Wolf of Badenoch*

Joan Beaufort = **James I**

James II = Mary *of Gueldres*

Margaret *of Denmark* = **James III**

James IV = Margaret Tudor = 2 Archibald Douglas, *Earl of Angus*

Mary *of Guise* = **James V**   Margaret Douglas = *Earl of Lennox*

Mary *Queen of Scots* = Henry Stewart, *Lord Darnley*

James VI and I *of England*

16. James I was the first Scottish king of whom a reasonably reliable likeness survives. This image was painted in the sixteenth century, one of a set of the first five Jameses, but it may reflect a contemporary work. Panel, $16\frac{1}{4} \times 13$ in (41×33 cm). Detail. Scottish National Portrait Gallery, Edinburgh

James I

b. *c.* 1394; r. **1406-37**

Son of Robert III, who was the second of the Stewart kings, he succeeded at about twelve years of age. In 1424 he was crowned in Edinburgh after his release from eighteen years of captivity, during which time he was held at the English court while his uncle, the Duke of Albany, ruled Scotland. He grew close to Henry V, who was more of a friend than gaoler (it was Henry IV who had first imprisoned him). He returned to Scotland with an English wife, Joan Beaufort, granddaughter of John of Gaunt, and in her praise wrote the famous love poem *The King's Quhair* (*The King's Book*). He was a firm ruler, too much so for some of his nobles who assassinated him in Perth in 1437.

James II

b. 1431; r. **1437-60**

James was crowned at the age of six. He was married to Mary of Gueldres. On coming of age he set about reducing the power of the nobles. He was a strong and vigorous ruler who dealt firmly with the treachery of his lords, even to the point of killing one (William Douglas) himself in a fit of rage. He was known to be a brave warrior and was killed by an explosion from one of his own cannons while besieging Roxburgh Castle.

17. *Right:* James II (detail). Like his father's portrait, this is one of a sixteenth-century set but perhaps based on an earlier image, although it does not show the facial birthmark for which he was known as 'James of the Fiery Face'. Panel, $16\frac{1}{4} \times 13$ in (41×33 cm). Scottish National Portrait Gallery

18. James III by Hugo van der Goes. This picture portrays him with his son, afterwards James IV (the boy's identity has been questioned but this is the most likely solution). The left-hand wing, probably for a triptych of which the centre panel is now lost, was commissioned for the Collegiate Church of the Holy Trinity, Edinburgh. c. 1475. Panel, 78 × 38 in (198.5 × 97 cm). Royal Collection, on loan to the National Gallery of Scotland, Edinburgh

James III

b. 1452; r. **1460-88**

James III's reign was tempestuous and ended in his assassination by an unknown hand after the battle of Sauchieburn against the rebellious Homes. Ironically, he had an easy-going temperament and a marked distaste for military affairs, thereby undoing much of the work of his father and grandfather. He married Margaret of Denmark, a beautiful, virtuous and loyal wife. He was not greatly loved by his subjects and indeed was several times faced with rebellion: on one of these occasions the lords were led by the Earl of Angus, called 'Bell-the-Cat' because he volunteered to beard the king with an ultimatum.

19. The James III silver groat, c. 1485, here greatly enlarged, was 'probably the earliest Renaissance coin portrait outside Italy'. National Museum of Antiquities of Scotland, Edinburgh

James IV

b. 1473; r. **1488-1513**

At the age of fifteen the boy was captured by his father's enemies and forced to follow them at the battle of Sauchieburn. As a result he was pursued by remorse for the rest of his life, feeling an association of guilt for his father's murder. As a king he was a consolidator of internal peace and patron of learning; he earned the praise of the scholar Erasmus and under his influence the Scottish arts flourished (as, for example, in the poetry of William Dunbar and Robert Henryson). He took up the cause of Perkin Warbeck, pretender to the English throne, and sheltered him for a while. He had a beautiful mistress, Margaret Drummond, who died mysteriously and suddenly just before his marriage in 1503 to Margaret Tudor, daughter of Henry VII. It was through a descendant of this match that the crowns of England and Scotland were united exactly a century later. He was slain in 1513 at the battle of Flodden against the English.

IACOBVS.QVINTVS.SCOTTORVM.REX ⚜
ANNO.ÆTATIS.SVE.

MARIA.LOTHORINGIA.ILLIVS.IN.SECVNDIS.NVP
TIIS.VXOR.ANNO ÆTATIS SVE. Z 4 ⚜

22. *Above:* James V and his wife Mary of Guise. The image of James is similar to that known in other portraits. 43 × 56½ in (109 × 143.5 cm). National Trust, Hardwick Hall

21. *Left:* Margaret Tudor by Daniel Mytens (detail). An early seventeenth-century painting based on a contemporary head and shoulders portrait. Oil on canvas, 94 × 55½ in (239 × 141 cm). Royal Collection, Holyrood House, Edinburgh

20. *Far left:* James IV. This is one of the sixteenth-century set of portraits of the first five Jameses. Panel, 16¼ × 13 in (41 × 33 cm). Scottish National Portrait Gallery

Margaret Tudor

1489-1541

The daughter of Henry VII, at the age of fifteen Margaret married James IV of Scotland. It was through her that her great-grandson James VI eventually inherited the English throne as James I. After her husband's death, she assumed the regency of Scotland, aided by Archbishop Beaton and the Earls of Huntly, Angus and Arran. Her influence, however, gradually declined, and the return from France of the Duke of Albany, the next in line to the throne after her sons, caused a split between her supporters and his. When in 1514 she married Archibald Douglas, Earl of Angus, she alienated many of the lords, who replaced her as regent by Albany. Her daughter by Angus, Lady Margaret Douglas, became Countess of Lennox and the mother of Lord Darnley. Later she divorced Angus and in 1528 married Henry Stewart, later Lord Methven.

James V

b. 1512; r. **1513-42**

James succeeded his father at the tender age of eighteen months. The Duke of Albany, James III's nephew, ousted Queen Margaret from the regency and held the position himself until James was crowned king at sixteen. He was given the Order of the Garter by Henry VIII, whose attempts to persuade him to follow the reformed religion he resisted. His first marriage was to Madeleine, the daughter of François I of France, who died within six months. His second wife was Mary of Guise-Lorraine, widow of the Duc de Longueville. He had numerous bastard children. Greed prompted him to seize the lands of many of his enemies – largely Douglases. He died of no apparent cause but a broken heart after the defeat by the English at Solway Moss. When his daughter Mary was born he is recorded as saying of the throne, 'It cam' wi' a lass, it will pass wi' a lass', referring to Marjorie, daughter of Robert the Bruce who by marrying Walter the Steward founded the Stewart (or Stuart) line of kings.

MARIE
REINE
ESCOS
SE

23. Mary Queen of Scots by an unknown artist. Oil on canvas, 38 × 24½ in (96.5 × 62 cm). Forster Bequest, Victoria and Albert Museum

Mary Queen of Scots

b. 1542; r. **1542-67;** d. 1587

Born into a conflict over Scotland between France and England, Mary succeeded her father James V when she was only a few days old. She was sent to the French court to be brought up and there acquired the French manners which later made it so difficult for her to accommodate herself to the rough Scots lords. At the age of sixteen she married the Dauphin of France, the son of Henri II and Catherine de Medici; he died a year and a half after succeeding as François II. Regarded by Catholics as the rightful heir to the English throne (Elizabeth being, in their eyes, illegitimate), she returned to Scotland to find that the country had turned Protestant, with John Knox fulminating from the pulpit against her and the Catholic church. In 1565 she married her cousin Henry Stewart, Lord Darnley, a weak, vicious but handsome man. He was killed by an explosion at Kirk O'Field (now the site of Edinburgh University Old Quad). Popular myth blamed Mary and James Hepburn, Earl of Bothwell, for his death, but she is unlikely to have been responsible. She subsequently married Bothwell – one of the few Scots lords whom she felt to be on her side. It was said that she was passionately in love with him, but it may well have been that she was raped by him and felt obliged to marry him to preserve her honour. In 1567 she was imprisoned on Loch Leven and forced to abdicate in favour of James, her son by Darnley. She later escaped and fled to England, where she was taken prisoner and held for nineteen years (mostly at Sheffield) before Elizabeth eventually (and reluctantly) had her beheaded. The length of her actual reign was only about seven years, but the romance of her tempestuous life – either as tragic heroine or licentious murderess – has animated both literature and legend.

24. *Right:* Mary Queen of Scots, drawing by François Clouet. c. 1560–61. Bibliothèque Nationale, Paris

25. *Far right:* Mary Queen of Scots, miniature by Nicholas Hilliard. c. 1578. 2 × 1½ in (5 × 4 cm). Victoria and Albert Museum

SAXON KINGS

26. Offa: this silver penny, here much enlarged, bearing his profile and name was struck by the Canterbury moneyer Abba and may have been an attempt at a likeness. National Portrait Gallery

27. Alfred: this silver penny, also enlarged, was struck by the Canterbury moneyer Heahstan. National Portrait Gallery

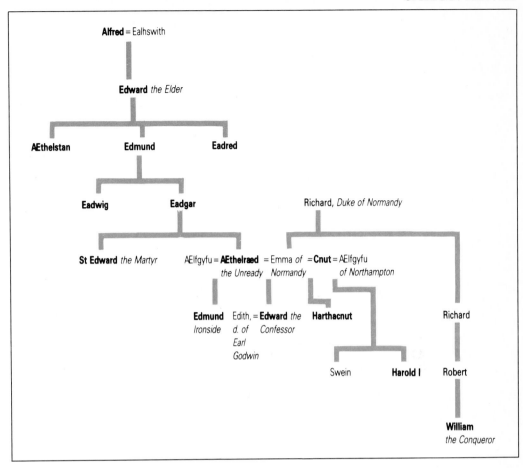

Offa

r. **757-96**

A major figure amongst the early English kings, Offa, King of Mercia (the central kingdom of England), won sovereignty over all of England south of the Humber. He was the first to call himself 'king of the English'. He was regarded by Charlemagne as an equal – the only Western leader to be so privileged – and considered himself as the successor of the Saxon 'Bretwaldas', high kings of Britain, overlords of all the smaller kingdoms. His attempts to establish a dynasty foundered when his son Ecgfrith died shortly after him; about a quarter of a century later the kings of Wessex took supremacy. He was responsible for Offa's Dyke, an extensive earthwork along the boundary of the Welsh kingdom. In his reign the first silver currency was introduced.

Alfred

b. 849; r. **871-99**

The youngest of the six children of Æthelwulf, king of Wessex, Alfred became the most famous and illustrious of all the early English kings. Wessex was then the only English kingdom holding out against the Danes, who had first invaded on a massive scale in 865. After another great invasion in 878 Alfred retired to 'Egbert's Stone' (probably in Somerset) to build up his army where, as the story goes, he inadvertently allowed some cakes to burn while attending to his weapons by a fire. He subsequently defeated the Danes (whose king Guthrum was then duly baptized), reorganized the Wessex defences and built ships to contain the Danish menace. Sickly, moody and anxious by temperament, he managed by great efforts of will to overcome these disabilities, as well as his early ignorance and illiteracy, to become not only a great soldier and statesman, but also a considerable scholar. He enjoyed learning and the company of intellectuals, and both translated himself and had translated many works of philosophy, religion and history.

Æthelstan

r. 924-39

Æthelstan was the son of Edward the Elder, king of England from 901 to 924, and the grandson of Alfred the Great. He was brought up in Mercia and therefore commanded the loyalty of that kingdom as well as that of Wessex. He was victor over both the Scots – at the battle of Brunanburh – and the Vikings. In his reign considerable progress was made towards the unification of the English people; and both Scotland and Wales recognized his superiority. He was a devout king and, for his time, a humane legislator. He collected books, works of art and relics of saints from all over Europe. He was also a very generous patron of the arts and of the church.

Eadgar

b. 943; r. 959-75

Acknowledged as king of all England when he was only sixteen (he was Æthelstan's nephew), Eadgar held the throne in peace and prosperity. For his promotion of the peaceful union of the Danes and the English he was known as Eadgar the Pacific. He ruled with strength and wisdom and was guided by the advice of three great clerics – Dunstan, Oswald and Æthelwold – who also chronicled his reign. He supported the revival of learning and the reform of the monasteries led by these three men, all of whom were later canonized. A contemporary chronicler has left a striking and vivid record of his coronation ceremony, some elements of which were used at the coronation of Elizabeth II. His sons were Æthelræd the Unready (so-called from the Anglo-Saxon word 'Redeless', meaning 'ill-advised' or 'without counsel') and Edward, known as the Martyr and canonized following his murder at Corfe Castle by the followers of his brother (who was only a young boy at the time).

30. *Right:* Eadgar is shown here saluting saints, the heavenly host and Christ as majesty figure blessing from a mandorla, in an illumination in his manuscript charter to the New Minster at Winchester in 966. British Library, Cotton Ms Vesp. A.viii, fol. 2v

28. Aethelstan, in this illustration from the manuscript *Life of St Cuthbert* by Bede c. 930, is shown crowned but humbly offering the book to the saint himself. Corpus Christi, Cambridge, Ms 183, fol. iv

29. *Left:* Aethelstan: silver penny (enlarged). Mrs R.C. Lockett Collection

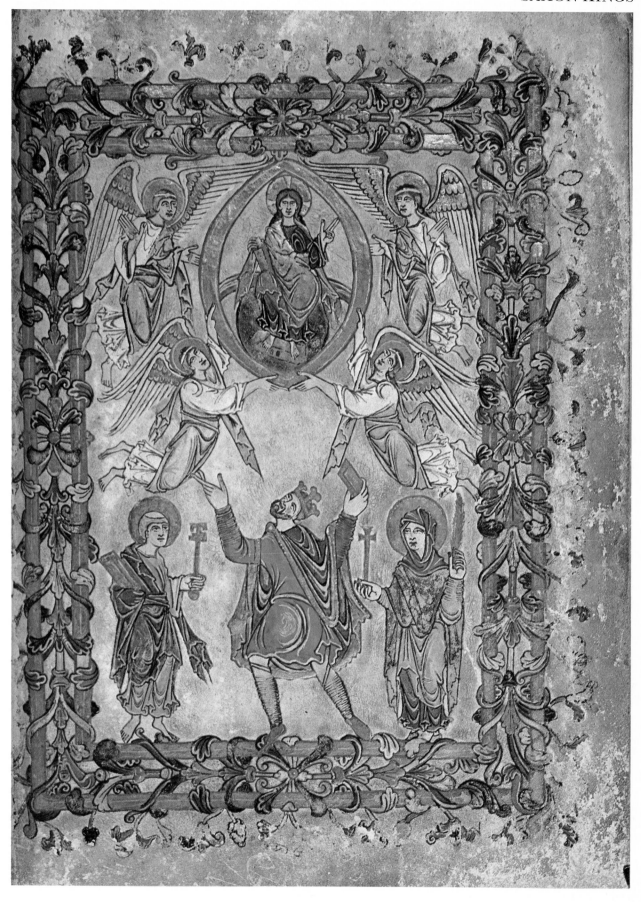

Cnut

r. 1016-35

Cnut was the son of the Danish king Swein whose landing in England in 1013, following a period of persistent invasion and attack throughout Æthelræd's reign, brought the final submission of the whole of England. After his father's death Cnut was chosen to be king in 1016 over the claims of Æthelræd's son Edmund Ironside. Cnut was at the same time king of Denmark and Norway and overlord of Sweden. A much feared and respected man, he ruthlessly removed any claimant to the throne and imposed his authority on Danes and English alike. Holinshed tells the famous story of how he had himself carried to the edge of the sea and commanded the tide to stop; only as it lapped over his feet did he concede that his power did not extend over the elements. He married Æthelræd's widow Emma of Normandy and also had a 'temporary queen', Ælfgyfu of Northampton, with whom he ruled in Denmark. By the former he had a son, Harthacnut, and by the latter a son who became Harold I.

31. Cnut, manuscript illumination. British Museum, Cotton Ms Claudius D.II, f.20

Edward the Confessor

b. c. 1004; r. 1042-66

The son of Æthelræd and Emma, Edward was in exile until the death of his half-brother Harthacnut (who succeeded Harold I in 1040). Having been brought up without any expectation of succeeding to the throne (although shortly before he died Harthacnut probably designated him as his successor), he had neither the appetite nor the ability suitable for the office. His most notable characteristics were a love of hunting and a great piety; he was the founder of Westminster Abbey and was later canonized. He married Edith, the daughter of the most powerful noble in the kingdom, Earl Godwin, whose high-handedness and arrogance drove Edward in due course to exile him. Having promised the throne to William of Normandy, Edward was later forced to receive Earl Godwin back into favour and eventually nominated his most outstanding son, Harold, to succeed him.

32. Edward the Confessor, silver penny (enlarged). Corporation of London

33, 34. Edward the Confessor's first Great Seal has a version of the majesty figure on both sides. Actual size (approx.). Westminster Abbey Library

Harold II

b. 1022; r. **1066**

The last years of Edward the Confessor left the question of succession in some confusion. Both Harold, Earl Godwin's son, and William of Normandy claimed that the throne had been promised them by Edward; and the most famous Viking warrior, Harald Hardrada, king of Norway, was also laying claim. On Edward's death Harold was proclaimed king. In his favour was the fact that he had been in charge of the army under the old king and was considered strong enough to resist Hardrada's threat of invasion from the north; he had the support of the nobles and had endeared himself to Edward who found him less presumptuous than his father. When Hardrada launched an invasion Harold inflicted a crushing defeat on him at Stamford Bridge; by a twist of fate William of Normandy landed at Hastings two days later and Harold was once more plunged into battle, when he was killed. There is some doubt that the figure in the Bayeux Tapestry shot in the eye by an arrow is actually Harold.

35. Harold II, silver penny (enlarged). Corporation of London

NORMAN KINGS

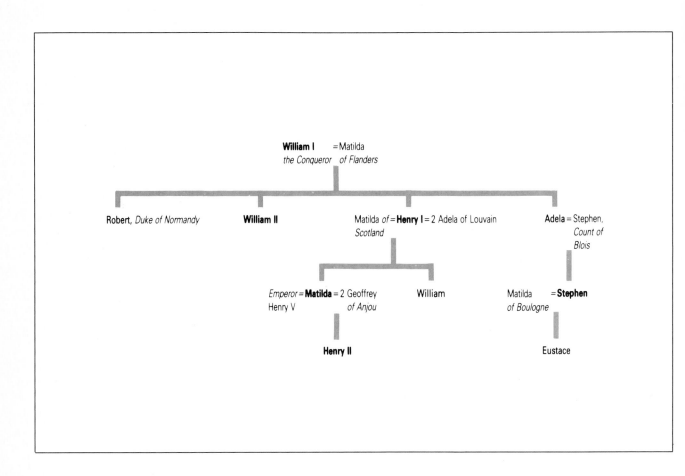

William I = Matilda
the Conqueror   of Flanders

Robert, *Duke of Normandy*   **William II**   Matilda *of* = **Henry I** = 2 Adela of Louvain   Adela = Stephen,
                                                        Scotland   *Count of*
                                                                                                                Blois

Emperor = **Matilda** = 2 Geoffrey   William   Matilda   = **Stephen**
Henry V   *of Anjou*   *of Boulogne*

Henry II   Eustace

DINA NTES· ET·CVNAN· CLAVES·POR REXIT· HIC·WILLELM·
DEDIT· HAROLDO
ARMA

William I

b. 1027; r. **1066-87**

William was the illegitimate son of Robert II, Duke of Normandy, and Arlette (Herleva), daughter of William the Tanner. His half-brother was Odo, Bishop of Bayeux. His claim to the English throne rested on a promise to him by Edward the Confessor (who later changed his mind, probably under pressure from his nobles, and promised it to Harold instead) and a sworn oath – either of allegiance or assistance – by Harold himself, who had been captured when the wind blew his ship on to the French coast. There followed what was to be the most famous battle in English history, at Hastings. Having earned his title as The Conqueror for his invasion of England, William established a firm government marked by such undertakings as the Domesday survey in 1086, a grand record of all land tenure throughout the country. He also built the White Tower, the central portion of what is now the Tower of London. He married Matilda of Flanders, who was a descendant of Alfred the Great. Although Saxon unrest persisted throughout much of his reign, he eventually won over the last of the English leaders, Hereward the Wake.

36. *Below left:* this detail from the Bayeux Tapestry of about 1086 shows Harold II (on the right) being honoured by William of Normandy for his prowess in a campaign they fought together. Bayeux, France

39. *Below:* this detail from the Bayeux Tapestry shows William I at the Battle of Hastings, lifting his helmet to show his face and thus refute a rumour that he has been killed. Bayeux, France

37. *Above:* William I's Great Seal. The traditional imagery of the Great Seal, used to authenticate important documents in the name of the monarch, is established in the seal and counterseal: there is a majesty figure on one side (illustrated) and an equestrian warrior on the other. British Museum

38. *Below:* William I, silver penny (slightly enlarged) British Museum

William II

b. *c.* 1056; r. **1087-1100**

Known as Rufus, being red of face and possibly of hair, William was chosen by his father to succeed in England. His elder brother Robert, who was passed over (not without feeling considerable resentment), was given the dukedom of Normandy, which Rufus later had ambitions to wrest from him. Since the principle of hereditary right of succession was not as yet fully established, William Rufus thought it prudent to arrive in England with a letter confirming his father's wishes to the Archbishop of Canterbury, Lanfranc. His hostility to the church made him many enemies, and he earned a reputation – not wholly deserved – for blasphemy, licentiousness and villainy. While hunting in the New Forest, he was killed by an arrow said to have been shot by Sir Walter Tyrrell (or Tirel). Whether his death was an accident or a plot stage-managed by his brother Henry has never been satisfactorily resolved. He was buried in Winchester.

Henry I

b. 1068; r. **1100-35**

Henry was the youngest of William the Conqueror's three sons and came to the throne on the death of his brother William Rufus. The only son to have been 'born in the purple', that is after his father became king, he assumed that this gave him greater entitlement to rule than his brothers. When Rufus died Henry galloped with indecent haste to Winchester to seize the royal treasure and without waiting to see his brother buried, sped on to Westminster where he was crowned within three days. His other brother Robert, on return from the Crusades, was presented with a *fait accompli*. Henry later also deprived Robert of the duchy of Normandy. He ruled both long and efficiently, but was capable also of great savagery and cruelty. On the other hand, because of his encouragement of scholars at court he earned the name 'Beauclerc', and the great Abbot Suger of St Denis was impressed by him. By his first wife Matilda of Scotland he had a son, William, on whom his dynastic hopes were pinned; these, however, were wrecked by William's death in the White Ship in 1120. He married for the second time Adela of Louvain, but the marriage was childless. Matilda was his only surviving legitimate child, although he had many illegitimate offspring.

40. William II, Great Seal. Actual size (approx.). Eton College, Berks

41. Henry I, silver penny (enlarged). F. Elmore Jones Collection

Stephen

b. *c.* 1097; r. **1135-54**

Stephen was the nephew of Henry I, with whom he was a great favourite, and on whose death he seized the crown, although Henry's daughter, the Empress Matilda, claimed it. He was the son of Henry's sister Adela and the Comte de Blois; he married Matilda of Boulogne. His reign was interrupted by bitter civil war between his own and Matilda's supporters. She had a brief success in 1141, but he soon regained the throne. He tried to ensure the succession for his son Eustace, but the Church was opposed to this and he was finally persuaded to leave the throne to Matilda's son Henry. An attractive, gallant and charming individual, as a king he was weak and somewhat unreliable; he lacked the strength to control his followers or subdue his enemies. He relied greatly on his brother Henry, who was made bishop of Winchester.

Matilda

1102-67

Matilda was born in 1102, the daughter of Henry I. At the age of twelve she married the Holy Roman Emperor Henry V and lived in the Empire (that is, in Germany) until his death in 1125. Although she had no wish to return to England, she was necessary to her father's political manoeuvres. In 1128 she married, reluctantly, Geoffrey, Count of Anjou (called Plantagenet because of his habit of decorating his hat with a sprig of broom – *Planta Genista*). With him she invaded England in 1135 to seize the throne from King Stephen; she captured the king in 1141 but was soon forced to exchange him for her illegitimate half-brother Robert of Gloucester. Stephen regained the crown and thereafter her power dwindled. She escaped from her imprisonment in Oxford Castle through the snow and stayed in the West Country for five years, before retiring to Normandy where she died in 1167.

42. Stephen, silver penny (enlarged). British Museum

43. Matilda, silver penny (enlarged) (probably with the features of King Stephen). Coins and portraits of the Empress are almost unknown. British Museum

THE PLANTAGENETS

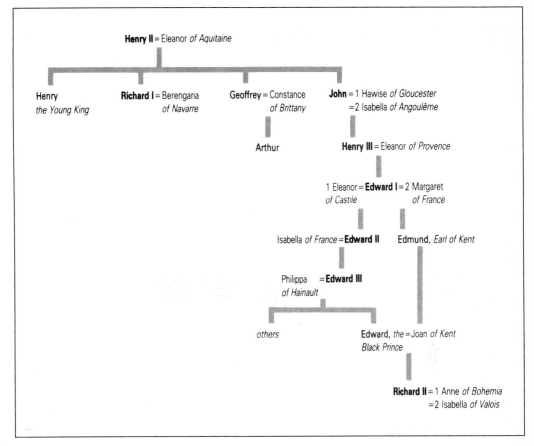

Henry II = Eleanor *of Aquitaine*

Henry
the Young King

Richard I = Berengaria
of Navarre

Geoffrey = Constance
of Brittany

Arthur

John = 1 Hawise *of Gloucester*
= 2 Isabella *of Angoulême*

Henry III = Eleanor *of Provence*

1 Eleanor = **Edward I** = 2 Margaret
of Castile   *of France*

Isabella *of France* = **Edward II**   Edmund, *Earl of Kent*

Philippa   = **Edward III**
of Hainault

others

Edward, *the* = Joan *of Kent*
Black Prince

Richard II = 1 Anne *of Bohemia*
= 2 Isabella *of Valois*

44. *Left:* Henry II's effigy in Fontevrault is retrospective (probably early thirteenth century) but there may be some attempt at a likeness, although the features are clearly fairly generalized. Fontevrault Abbey, Chinon, France

45. Henry II with Thomas à Becket, manuscript illumination. British Museum, Royal Ms 20 A II, f.76

Henry II

b. 1133; r. **1154-89**

Son of Matilda and Geoffrey, Henry II inherited Anjou and Normandy, and by marrying Eleanor, the divorced wife of Louis VII of France, he also acquired Aquitaine. He was a strong and active ruler who resolved the troubles of the previous reign. His reputation, however, is clouded by his involvement in the murder of Thomas à Becket. Having given his intimate friend and Chancellor the archbishopric of Canterbury, he found that Becket adopted an unyielding position in defence of the church's privileges. Their disagreement was strong and bitter until Henry's exasperation was taken by four knights to be a command, and they assassinated Becket on the steps of his own cathedral. For this Henry did penance for the rest of his life, and he built a great shrine at Canterbury in honour of Becket. He had four sons: Henry, Richard, Geoffrey and John; Henry was crowned in his father's lifetime and was known as the Young King. Before he died in 1183 the Young King, joined by his brothers Richard and John (Geoffrey also died young), rebelled with their mother against their father, and this was a shattering blow to Henry.

Eleanor, Duchess of Aquitaine

1122-1204

Eleanor was the granddaughter of Guillaume d'Aquitaine – one of the first troubadours – and heiress to great lands. She was famous for her beauty and cultivated mind and was, more than anyone else, responsible for making fashionable the cult of courtly love that flourished in the twelfth and thirteenth centuries. Her first marriage was to the saintly, but dull, Louis VII of France. After her divorce she married Henry II, a few years her junior, and as his wife presided over a brilliant court. In later years they fell out. For inciting her sons to rebellion Eleanor was imprisoned in 1174 and kept in Salisbury for thirteen years. At the age of about eighty she travelled to Spain to attend the wedding of her granddaughter Blanche of Castile to Louis VIII of France, heir to Philippe Auguste. She later retired to the abbey of Fontevrault, where she died.

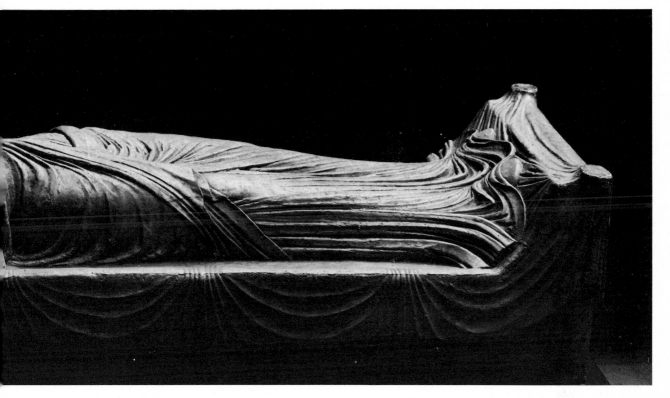

46. *Above:* Eleanor of Aquitaine, effigy in Fontevrault. Again, this is a somewhat generalized image. Chinon, France

Richard I

b. 1157; r. **1189-99**

Richard was the second surviving son of Henry II, and was known as Cœur-de-Lion for his bravery as a warrior. His reputation as a good king was probably undeserved: less than a year of his reign was spent in England, a country for which he had little love, being more at home in France. He was given the lands of Aquitaine by his mother and the duchy of Normandy by his father. His queen was Berengaria of Navarre. He was one of the leaders of the third crusade in 1190 and he dreamed of liberating Jerusalem from the Infidel; he never, however, succeeded in entering the town. Richard and the Muslim leader Saladin held each other in mutual respect and their chivalrous conduct to one another became legendary. On the crusade Richard and the French king, Philippe Auguste, formerly partners in rebellion against Henry II, quarrelled; Richard also insulted Leopold of Austria. On his way home he was captured by the Emperor and held until he was discovered, as the legend goes, by the troubadour Blondel. He was ransomed at great cost to his subjects. He was killed at the siege of Chaluz in France.

47. *Left:* Richard I's monumental stone effigy was made presumably at the same time as that of his father and mother alongside: the likeness is doubtful and has nothing in common with another effigy of Richard at Rouen. Fontevrault Abbey, Chinon, France

48. *Left:* bruised in nose and mouth, John's effigy retains still an impressive dignity. Worcester Cathedral

John

b. 1167; r. **1199-1216**

The youngest and favourite son of Henry II, John was nicknamed 'Lackland' because all his father's territories were parcelled out among his elder brothers; nevertheless he joined them in revolt against Henry. After his brother Richard's death it is probable that he disposed of his nephew Arthur of Brittany, Geoffrey's son, who had a good claim to the throne. His first wife was Hawise of Gloucester, his second, Isabella of Angoulême. He was continually at war either at home or in France – he lost Normandy to the French. He also quarrelled with the Pope and was excommunicated. He was oppressive and grasping, but his faults have been to some extent exaggerated. The Magna Carta presented to him by his discontented barons in 1215 – a document, in fact, which did more to protect the rights of barons than to offer a charter of liberty for his common subjects – represented a significant step towards the limitation of monarchical power. At the end of his life he sustained a serious blow when, in the course of a campaign, his treasure train was lost in the muddy estuary of the Wash.

Henry III

b. 1207; r. **1216-72**

The son of John and Isabella of Angoulême, Henry came to the throne as a boy of nine. He married Eleanor of Provence. Although he confirmed Magna Carta, he was beset by the continuing revolt of the barons. In 1258 there was open rebellion led by Simon de Montfort, who had come to represent popular aspirations to liberty and good government. De Montfort summoned local leaders from all over the country to air grievances and to demand a fairer framework of local laws, thus laying the foundations for a regular gathering of barons and commoners which in the next reign developed into the earliest parliament. In 1265 Simon de Montfort was killed at the battle of Evesham. Although Henry reigned for more than fifty years he was not popular, partly because he favoured his wife's French relatives over his English nobles. He was responsible for rebuilding Westminster Abbey.

49. *Right:* Henry III's gilt-bronze effigy by William Torel was commissioned by his son Edward I in 1291 and is clearly idealized. It is close in feeling to the Fontevrault effigies of almost a century earlier. Westminster Abbey

Edward I

b. 1239; r. **1272-1307**

The most praised of all mediaeval kings, Edward was a great soldier, pacifier and initiator of constitutional and parliamentary reform. Although he never succeeded in finally subduing the Scots – he was unable to overcome the patriotic fervour aroused by William Wallace – his persistence earned him the name of Hammer of the Scots. He also took the Stone of Scone, upon which the kings of Scotland had always been crowned, to Westminster, where it remains. He conquered much of Wales and proclaimed his son the first English Prince of Wales. From his Welsh campaigns he learnt the use of the longbow and thus built up the famous army of archers which was so successful throughout the fourteenth century. He also fostered and reorganized the 'parliament' that had developed in his father's day, and reformed the laws of tenancy and property. He married Eleanor of Castile. When she died, his grief moved him to build a cross at each resting stage of the bier's journey from Lincoln to London; some are still standing. Later he married Margaret of France.

50. *Left:* Edward I, a nineteenth-century engraving from a statue formerly at Caernarvon. Mansell Collection

51. *Right:* Edward I, drawing from a Memorandum Roll. Public Record Office, London

52. *Far right:* Eleanor of Castile, effigy in Westminster Abbey

Edward II

b. 1284; r. **1307-27**

A weak and ineffectual king and a disastrous soldier, Edward, a homosexual, was dominated by favourites such as the young commoner Piers Gaveston, who was executed by his barons, and later Hugh le Despenser (Spenser). He was routed by Robert the Bruce at Bannockburn in 1314 and never recovered his losses in Scotland. He married Isabella of France, daughter of Philip IV, later known as the She-Wolf. His vacillations and lack of leadership eventually led to his being deposed by the barons led by Roger Mortimer, Earl of March, who was the queen's lover. Edward was then murdered in horrible fashion at Berkeley Castle on Isabella's and Mortimer's orders. He was buried in Gloucester Cathedral.

Edward III

b. 1312; r. **1327-77**

Edward came to the throne at the age of fourteen when his father, Edward II, was deposed and murdered. A few years later he sought out Mortimer and had him brutally executed; his mother was confined to a luxurious imprisonment. He married Philippa of Hainault, who proved a most popular queen. An ambitious and able soldier, Edward in 1337 launched the Hundred Years' War with France, claiming the right to the French throne through his mother although the French did not recognize the principle of inheritance through the female line. Edward had a famous victory with his archers at Crécy in 1346, but he was unable to consolidate his successes. Two years later the Black Death ravaged the country and well over one-third of the population died. Those who survived soon recognized that their contribution to the economic functioning of the country was indispensable and that they could therefore make political demands; thereafter the common people began to assert their rights. In 1348 Edward instituted the Order of the Garter, with its motto 'Honi soit qui mal y pense', supposedly said by Edward as he picked up the Countess of Salisbury's garter, which she had dropped while dancing with him.

53. The effigy of Edward II in Gloucester Cathedral is still obviously idealized, but is the most vigorous and splendid — despite *graffiti* scored on the face by vandals — of heads of early English royal effigies, although betraying little of the character attributed to him by disapproving historians

54. *Above:* Edward II penny (enlarged), from the Bury St Edmunds mint. Oxford, Ashmolean Museum

55. The serenely handsome head of Edward III's effigy has been said to be based on a death mask, and although surely smoothed out, indicates the age of the subject. Gilt-bronze, by John Orchard(?). Westminster Abbey

Edward, the Black Prince

1330-63

Edward was the eldest son of Edward III, and would have been king, but he died before his father, in 1363. He was known as the Black Prince possibly because he always wore black armour in battle. He was a great and famous warrior; he won an important victory over the French at Poitiers in 1356. He also led the so-called 'free companies', mercenary bands who could be recruited for war as long as there was a profit to be made from looting. He married Joan, the Fair Maid of Kent, daughter of Edmund, Earl of Kent, Edward I's son by his second marriage to Margaret of France.

56. Edward the Black Prince, electrotype of effigy in Canterbury Cathedral, c. 1377–80. Height 47 in (119 cm). National Portrait Gallery

57. In the three
portraits of Richard II
reproduced here and
on the following pages
it is clear for the first
time that a naturalistic
likeness is being
sought. This overlife-
size painting in
Westminster Abbey is
very much the
traditional figure of
majesty, but individual
features of the face
agree with those in the
Wilton Diptych and on
the effigy. Oil on
panel, 84 × 43 in
(213 × 109 cm).
Detail

59. *Above*: the copper effigy of Richard II and his queen, Anne of Bohemia, was ordered from Nicholas Broker and Godfrey Prest in 1395, five years before Richard died and so presumably approved by him. Westminster Abbey

58. *Left:* the Wilton Diptych — much argued about still — is certainly of the period, showing Richard II with his patron saints (including Edward the Confessor), as a young man in adoration of the Virgin amongst angels. This and the over life-size painting may be posthumous, but both clearly reflect an agreed image of what the king looked like in life. Wood, each panel 18 × 11½ in (46 × 29 cm). National Gallery

Richard II

b. 1367; r. **1377-99**

Son of the Black Prince, Richard inherited a land exhausted by war and financially drained by heavy taxation. When he was only fourteen, John Ball and Wat Tyler led the Peasants' Revolt of 1381 to protest against the exploitation of the working people, the imbalance of wealth and the clergy's excessive economic and political clout. Richard faced the rebels with courage and promised to meet some of their demands; but in the ensuing dispute Tyler was killed by one of the king's party. During his reign the Lollards and John Wycliffe were propagating heretical views against the doctrines of the Church. Richard, sensitive, cultivated and artistic, appreciated beauty and was a patron of Chaucer. He married Anne of Bohemia and was heart-broken when she died in 1394. He was deposed by his cousin Henry Bolingbroke, the future Henry IV, and died in prison in Pontefract.

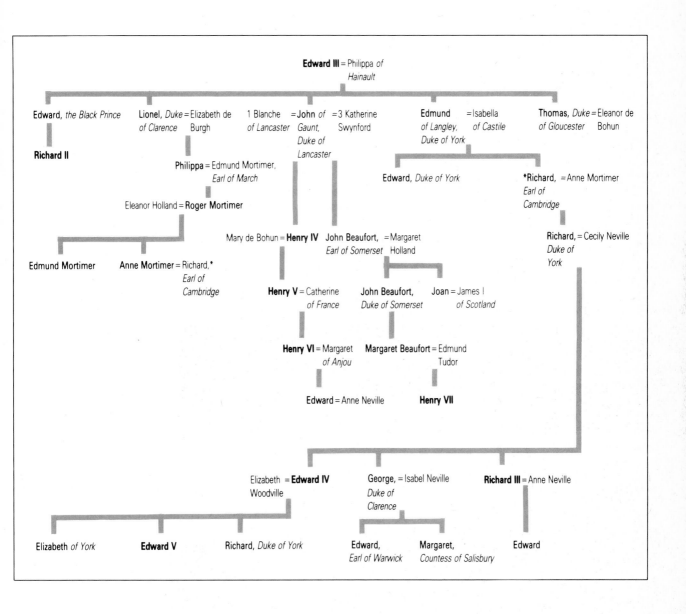

Edward III = Philippa *of Hainault*

Edward, *the Black Prince* — Lionel, *Duke of Clarence* = Elizabeth de Burgh — 1 Blanche *of Lancaster* = **John** *of Gaunt, Duke of Lancaster* = 3 Katherine Swynford — Edmund *of Langley, Duke of York* = Isabella *of Castile* — Thomas, *Duke of Gloucester* = Eleanor de Bohun

Richard II

Philippa = Edmund Mortimer, *Earl of March*

Edward, *Duke of York*

Richard, Earl of Cambridge = Anne Mortimer

Eleanor Holland = Roger Mortimer

Mary de Bohun = **Henry IV** — John Beaufort, *Earl of Somerset* = Margaret Holland

Richard, *Duke of York* = Cecily Neville

Edmund Mortimer — Anne Mortimer = Richard,* *Earl of Cambridge*

Henry V = Catherine *of France* — John Beaufort, *Duke of Somerset* — Joan = James I *of Scotland*

Henry VI = Margaret *of Anjou* — Margaret Beaufort = Edmund Tudor

Edward = Anne Neville — **Henry VII**

Elizabeth Woodville = **Edward IV** — George, *Duke of Clarence* = Isabel Neville — **Richard III** = Anne Neville

Elizabeth *of York* — **Edward V** — Richard, *Duke of York* — Edward, *Earl of Warwick* — Margaret, *Countess of Salisbury* — Edward

Henry IV

b. 1366; r. **1399-1413**

60. *Left:* the effigy of Henry IV in Canterbury Cathedral is not very individually characterized. The electrotype is in the National Portrait Gallery

Son of John of Gaunt (duke of Lancaster and third son of Edward III) and Blanche of Lancaster, Henry took advantage of the restlessness of the barons to promote his own cause against the king and his supporters. He eventually forced Richard to abdicate and became the first Lancastrian king. He was much troubled by the revolts of the Scottish and Welsh Lords of the Marches – in Wales he confronted Mortimer and the patriot Owen Glendower and in Northumberland the unruly Henry Percy. The Wars of the Roses were later to centre largely round the struggles of these lords, with their rival connections to the throne. He first married Mary de Bohun (who gave birth to the future Henry V) and later Joanna of Navarre.

61. *Left:* Henry V, profile portrait. Panel, 15 × 21½ in (39 × 54.5 cm). Society of Antiquaries, Burlington House, London

Henry V

b. 1387; r. **1413-22**

Henry was a highly able monarch in peace and a fine soldier in war, but he died of an unknown illness at the early age of thirty-five. He took over the reins of power before his father's death (probably with less contrast in his style than Shakespeare would have us believe), and pursued with vigour the war in France. After his celebrated victory against a superior force at Agincourt in 1415, he married Catherine, the daughter of King Charles VI. He had a close alliance with Philip the Good, duke of Burgundy, against the French, partly because of the wool trade with Flanders. Although the Treaty of Troyes gave Henry a promise of succession to the French throne, both he and Charles VI died in the same year and the Dauphin (later Charles VII) did not recognize the treaty. Catherine later married (or lived with) a Welsh knight, Owen Tudor, whose descendant was Henry VII.

62. Henry V accepting Occleve's poem, *De Regimine Principum*. This manuscript illumination seems to be contemporary and a depiction of an individual in serene gravity, rather than of a symbol. Page size 11½ × 7½ in (29 × 19 cm). British Museum, Arundel Ms 38 f.37

ye noble and myȝtty Prince excellent
my lord the Prince · o my lord gracious
I humble seruant and obedient
... to ȝour estate hye and glorious
Of whyche I am ful tendre and ful ȝelous
... recommaunde vnto ȝour worthynesse
With herte enter and spirit of meeknesse

Henry VI

b. 1421; r. **1422-61** and **1470-71**

Henry VI succeeded at the age of nine months. In 1461 he was proclaimed king of France in Paris, but at the same time the Dauphin was crowned Louis XI in Rheims. In Henry's reign the Hundred Years' War was ended with the loss of the whole of France (except for Calais), partly because he lost the support of Burgundy and partly because Joan of Arc had galvanized France into a revival of energy (1429-31). Henry had little taste for kingship and less for war; he was devout and scholarly. He had also inherited the mental instability of his grandfather Charles VI of France. He founded Eton College in 1440 and began on King's College Chapel in Cambridge. He married the forceful Margaret of Anjou, who was determined to keep Henry on the throne and to have their son Edward inherit; to these ends she herself led armies in the Wars of the Roses, the quarrel between the Houses of York and Lancaster which broke out in 1455. Henry was eventually manoeuvred into declaring Richard, Duke of York, his heir over his own son. After York's execution Henry was deposed by York's son (Edward IV); however, he regained the throne for a while with the help of Warwick. In 1471 he was again deposed and his son Prince Edward killed at the battle of Tewkesbury; Henry was murdered by the Yorkist faction, probably on the orders of Edward IV.

63. This image of Henry VI was also widely circulated in the sixteenth-century set of royal portraits and although posthumous, probably has some close relationship to the king's appearance in life. Panel, 22 × 14 in (56.5 × 35.5 cm). Royal Collection

Edward IV

b. 1442; r. **1461-70** and **1471-83**

With the help of his close friend and adviser, the king-maker Earl of Warwick, Edward, son

of Richard, Duke of York, and Cecily Neville, the 'Rose of Raby', defeated the Lancastrians, deposed Henry VI and established himself and the Yorkist line on the throne. He married a widow, Elizabeth Woodville, beautiful but not of noble birth; this move was considered disastrous by his advisers, who had hoped that he would make a secure and sensible dynastic alliance in Europe. Edward quarrelled with Warwick over this, and the Woodvilles became a powerful faction. When Warwick and the king's brother George, Duke of Clarence, turned Lancastrian in 1470, Edward was briefly deposed; after a resounding victory at Tewkesbury he was triumphantly reinstated in the following year. Clarence was executed, and legend has it that he drowned in malmsey wine. Edward was a handsome and able man, pleasure-loving and popular, as well as a shrewd and brave soldier; he would, however, have been an even more effective monarch had it not been for his fault of self-indulgence. Under his patronage Caxton's printing press was set up at Westminster.

64. Portraits of Edward V are almost non-existent, but here he appears with his father and mother; the king is receiving a book from Earl Rivers and Caxton. The image of Edward IV agrees well with that in the standard painting of him. He originally owned this manuscript. *Dictes and Sayings of the Philosophers*, Lambeth Palace Library, Ms 265

65. Elizabeth Woodville, wife of Edward IV. $22\frac{1}{2} \times 16\frac{1}{2}$ in (57×42 cm). Queens' College, Cambridge

K.Edward 9 4th.

Edward V

b. 1471; r. **1483**

Edward's reign lasted only a few months. He was imprisoned at the age of twelve with his brother Richard, Duke of York, by their uncle Richard, Duke of Gloucester (later Richard III). The 'Princes in the Tower' then disappeared and at the time were both presumed murdered by Richard; however, there are conflicting views about this. In the reign of Henry VII two pretenders appeared: one of them, Perkin Warbeck, said he had been sent to Flanders before Bosworth and was in fact Richard, Duke of York. In spite of Perkin's attempt to stage a military rising the claim was derided by Henry and Perkin was hanged at Tyburn.

Margaret Beaufort

1443-1509

Descended from John of Gaunt through his third marriage to Katherine Swynford, she was the daughter of John, Duke of Somerset. She first married Edmund Tudor, Earl of Richmond; their only son became Henry VII. After Richmond's death she married Henry Stafford, son of the Duke of Buckingham. Her third husband was Thomas Stanley, Earl of Derby, whose defection from Richard III at Bosworth assured Henry's victory. She was learned and pious, and a major benefactress of colleges at Cambridge and Oxford; but she was imbued with the pride common to all the Beaufort line. Anxious at all times to uphold the interests of her son, Henry Tudor, she was under considerable suspicion at the courts of Edward IV and Richard III.

67. Margaret Beaufort, mother of Henry VII. Panel, 27 × 21½ in (68.5 × 55 cm). National Portrait Gallery

66. Edward IV. This portrait, like that of Henry VI, was posthumous, but the likeness is confirmed by other portraits. Panel, 27 × 19 in (68.5 × 48 cm). Royal Collection

Richard III

b. 1452; r. **1483-85**

Richard was the youngest brother of Edward IV and became the Protector of the young King Edward V; however, he declared his nephews illegitimate and took the throne shortly before Edward's coronation was due to take place. He was hated by the Woodvilles, but was always fiercely loyal to his brother. Contention still surrounds his part in the disappearance of the young Edward and his brother Richard, and some historians have argued for his innocence. He probably had a slight physical deformity resulting from a sickly childhood, but his hunchback was certainly exaggerated by Shakespeare, who also gave him a wholeheartedly evil character against which to contrast the virtues of the Tudors who followed him. He married Anne Neville, daughter of the Earl of Warwick and widow of Prince Edward, son of Henry VI and Margaret of Anjou. His own son Edward died shortly after Richard was crowned. Displaying his customary bravery on the battlefield, he was cut down and killed by the forces of Henry Tudor at Bosworth Field, the last battle of the Wars of the Roses.

68. Richard III (detail). This portrait is the standard image found in the sixteenth-century sets of royal portraits. Panel, 22 × 14 in (56 × 36 cm). Royal Collection

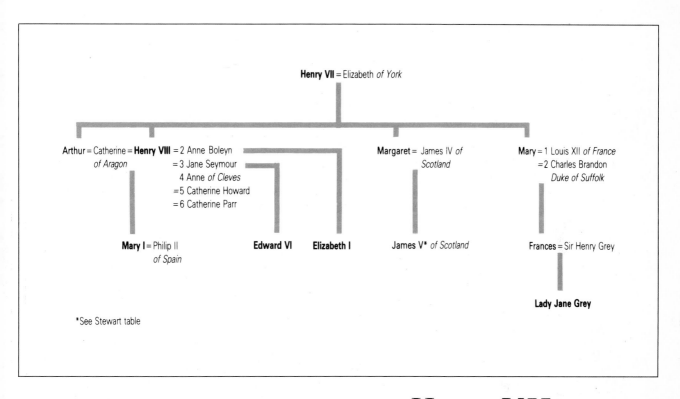

Henry VII = Elizabeth *of York*

Arthur = Catherine = **Henry VIII** = 2 Anne Boleyn
of Aragon   = 3 Jane Seymour
4 Anne *of Cleves*
= 5 Catherine Howard
= 6 Catherine Parr

Margaret = James IV *of Scotland*

Mary = 1 Louis XII *of France*
= 2 Charles Brandon
Duke of Suffolk

Mary I = Philip II *of Spain*

Edward VI   **Elizabeth I**

James V* *of Scotland*

Frances = Sir Henry Grey

Lady Jane Grey

*See Stewart table

Henry VII

b. 1457; r. **1485-1509**

Henry VII, first of the Tudor dynasty, was the son of the Lancastrian Earl of Richmond, Edmund Tudor (whose parents were the Welshman Owen Tudor and Catherine, widow of Henry V); his mother was the Plantagenet Margaret Beaufort. Through his mother he laid claim to the throne, and at Bosworth finally defeated the Yorkist forces. By marrying Elizabeth of York, the eldest daughter of Edward IV, he consolidated his own position and united the houses of York and Lancaster. He had Edward, Earl of Warwick, son of Clarence and nephew of both Edward IV and Richard III, executed, and dealt similarly with the pretenders Lambert Simnel and Perkin Warbeck, thereby removing the last surviving obstacles to his position. A remarkably able and crafty administrator, Henry restored peace and prosperity to England. He became known for careful, almost miserly management, sound law-making and somewhat chilly justice.

69. Gold sovereign of Henry VII. British Museum

Elizabeth of York

1465-1503

She was the eldest daughter of Edward IV, and sister of the Princes in the Tower; through her Yorkist blood her husband Henry VII was able to ensure possession of the throne. What had begun as a marriage of expedience, thought up by Elizabeth Woodville and Margaret Beaufort to buttress their positions vis-à-vis Richard III, developed into one of devoted companionship. The four surviving children of the marriage were Arthur, Prince of Wales (named in hope of a great new era), Henry VIII, Margaret (who married James IV of Scotland), and Mary who first married the French king Louis XII, and afterwards Charles Brandon, Duke of Suffolk, with whom she had always been in love; their grandchild was Lady Jane Grey.

72. *Above:* Elizabeth of York. Panel, 22 × 16½ in (56 × 42 cm). National Portrait Gallery

70. *Left:* Portraits of Henry VII illustrate very different angles of his personality. This small painting by M. Sittow, an international court painter, dates from 1505. 17 × 12 in (43 × 30 cm). National Portrait Gallery

71. Head of Henry VII's funeral effigy, almost certainly based on a death mask. The nose is a restoration. Westminster Abbey

Henry VIII

b. 1491; r. **1509-47**

The second son of Henry VII and Elizabeth, he became the heir after his brother Arthur's premature death in 1502. The first of his six marriages was to Arthur's widow, Catherine of Aragon, the daughter of Ferdinand and Isabella of Spain. Henry later used the closeness of this relationship to account for the absence of a male heir – he called it 'a cursed marriage'. The Pope's refusal to grant him a divorce caused him to break with Rome and to declare himself head of the Church in England. In hopes of a son he married Anne Boleyn, with whom he was passionately in love; his passion quickly faded and when he realized she would bear him no son, he had her executed on trumped-up charges of adultery. His next wife was Jane Seymour, a delicate woman who died after producing the longed-for boy. His three further wives were Anne of Cleves, Catherine Howard (a cousin of Anne Boleyn) and Catherine Parr who survived him. As a young prince he was brilliant, athletic and musical. After his quarrel with the Church, greed and near-absolute power turned him into a tyrant; in the end he was a bloated, diseased and hated figure. He was responsible for the dissolution of the monasteries and the seizure of their lands.

73, 74. The discrepancy between Henry VIII's appearance in youth and old age is encapsulated in his two armours: far left, of about 1512, and left, of about 1540. Tower of London

75. *Right:* Henry VIII, attributed to Joos van Cleve. Panel, $28\frac{1}{2}\times$ 23 in (72 × 58 cm). Royal Collection

76. The accepted image of Henry VIII is the great straddling whole-length by Hans Holbein the Younger, 1537; destroyed in the Whitehall fire of 1697, it is known by many copies such as this one. Oil on canvas, 92 × 53 in (234 × 135 cm). Walker Art Gallery, Liverpool

77. Catherine of Aragon (detail). Panel, 22 × 17½ in (56 × 44 cm). National Portrait Gallery

78. Anne Boleyn. Panel, 21½ × 16½ in (55 × 42 cm). National Portrait Gallery

79. Jane Seymour, by Holbein. c. 1536–7. Oil on panel, 25½ × 16 in (65 × 41 cm). Kunsthistorisches Museum, Vienna

80. Anne of Cleves, by Holbein. 1539. 25½ × 19 in (65 × 48 cm). Louvre, Paris

KATHARINE PARRE

82. *Right*: Edward VI, aged about five. After Holbein. c. 1542. Panel, 17 × 12 in (43 × 30 cm). National Portrait Gallery

Edward VI

81. *Left:* Catherine Parr (detail), attributed to William Scrots. c. 1545. Panel, 25 × 20 in (64 × 51 cm). National Portrait Gallery

b. 1537; r. **1547-53**

Edward, son of Henry VIII and Jane Seymour – Henry's only legitimate son – succeeded his father at the age of nine, but, always sickly, died of consumption at sixteen. He ruled precociously with the aid of the Protector, his uncle the Duke of Somerset. In his reign the Protestant Reformation, and iconoclasm, accelerated, and some of the worst excesses of the dissolution of the monasteries took place. Solemn and clever, Edward was a keen upholder of the new faith, but was probably not able to exercise much control over his nobles or the running of the affairs of state.

83. *Left:* Edward VI as a child, by Holbein. 1538. Wood, 22½ × 17½ in (57 × 44 cm). National Gallery, Washington DC – Andrew W. Mellon Coll.

84. *Below:* Mary I (detail) by 'Master John', 1544. Panel, 28 × 20 in (71 × 51 cm). National Portrait Gallery

85. *Right:* Mary I, by Anthonis Mor, 1554. Oil on panel, 43 × 33 in (109 × 84 cm). Prado, Madrid

Mary I

b. 1516; r. **1553-58**

Born in 1516, the eldest daughter of Henry VIII, Mary succeeded her half-brother Edward after the tragic episode of Lady Jane Grey, the 'Nine Days' Queen', who was placed on the throne by the Protestant faction. She was immediately deposed and later executed. On her accession Mary, a staunch Catholic, restored the old religion, reinforced in her determination by the harsh treatment meted out to her mother, Catherine of Aragon. By her marriage in 1554 to Philip II of Spain (whose beard Drake later threatened to singe) she created a powerful Catholic alliance. The marriage was not a success, however, and Philip returned to Spain the following year. There were no children (although there was at least one phantom pregnancy) and this caused her great unhappiness. The burning and execution of many Protestant 'heretics' earned her the sobriquet 'Bloody Mary' and the hatred of her subjects. Isolated and embittered, she died convinced of the rightness of her actions, a sad and lonely figure.

86, 87. Two miniatures of Elizabeth I by Nicholas Hilliard: the earlier (*left*), of 1572, is a fairly literal account of a woman of about forty (National Portrait Gallery); the later one (*right*), of the 1590s, is entirely idealized into a 'mask of beauty' (Victoria and Albert Museum)

Elizabeth I

b. 1533; r. **1558-1603**

The daughter of Henry VIII and Anne Boleyn, the greatest and last of the Tudors succeeded her half-sister Mary. Protestant by upbringing, she was immediately careful not to antagonize Catholics by outlawing the old faith. After a difficult childhood, in which her life was constantly menaced, she rose triumphantly to be called Gloriana – one of the most celebrated and acclaimed monarchs of all time, with a legendary ability to rule. She refused to marry, in spite of numerous pro-posed matches; she was said to be in love with Robert Dudley, Earl of Leicester (whose wife Amy Robsart was reputedly murdered be-cause of this) and later Robert Devereux, Earl of Essex, who was beheaded for treason. She fired her fleet with enthusiasm at Tilbury to repel the Spanish Armada in 1588: 'Though I have but the body of a weak and feeble woman, yet I have the heart and stomach of a king, and a king of England too'. She gave encourage-ment to Drake and Raleigh in their naval ventures. Always proud and haughty, as well as exceedingly wily, she refused to admit to ageing; the decrepitude of later years was masked by jewels and paint.

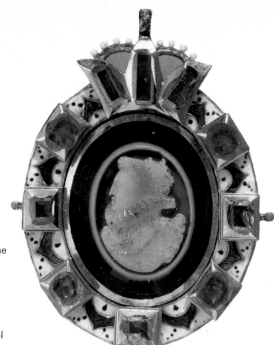

88. *Right*: Elizabeth I, the Barber jewel (detail). The cameo is almost the badge of a saint, worn for protection and veneration. Victoria and Albert Museum

89. *Below: Elizabeth I confounding the Three Goddesses*, by Hans Eworth, an allegory in which the queen surpasses Juno, Minerva and Venus in beauty. 1569. Panel, 28 × 33 in (71 × 84 cm). Royal Collection, Hampton Court, Middlesex

90. *Right*: Marcus Gheeraert's famous painting of Elizabeth I shows her as the figurehead, or very ship of state itself, of England, victor of the Armada. 1592. Canvas, 95 × 60 in (241 × 152 cm). National Portrait Gallery

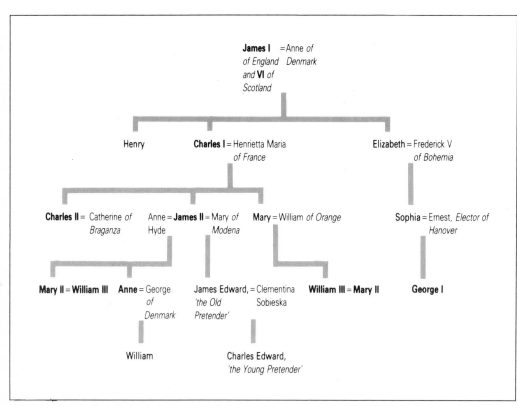

James I = Anne of
of England   Denmark
and VI of
Scotland

Henry   Charles I = Henrietta Maria   Elizabeth = Frederick V
of France   of Bohemia

Charles II = Catherine of   Anne = James II = Mary of   Mary = William of Orange   Sophia = Ernest, Elector of
Braganza   Hyde   Modena   Hanover

Mary II = William III   Anne = George   James Edward, = Clementina   William III = Mary II   George I
of   'the Old   Sobieska
Denmark   Pretender'

William   Charles Edward,
'the Young Pretender'

93. James I, miniature
by Nicholas Hilliard,
1603/8. Royal
Collection

91. *Far left:* Anne of
Denmark, wife of
James I, by P. van
Somer (detail). Oil on
canvas, 104½ × 82 in
(266 × 208 cm).
Royal Collection

92. *Left:* Henry, Prince
of Wales, by R. Peake,
c. 1610. Canvas, 68 ×
45 in (173 × 114 cm).
National Portrait
Gallery

THE STUARTS (STEWARTS)
AFTER JAMES I AND VI

James I
of England
James VI
of Scotland

b. 1566; r. from **1567** in Scotland; **1603-25** in both countries

James became King of Scotland at the age of one year, after his mother Mary Queen of Scots was deposed. On Elizabeth Tudor's death in 1603 he became the first of the Stuart kings of England; he succeeded through his great-grandmother Margaret, the daughter of Henry VII, as Elizabeth had no closer heirs. He was intelligent, acute and obstinate; he was also unmannerly and coarse. He was once described as 'the wisest fool in Christendom'; he was a firm believer in the divine right of kings to rule above the law. He was also strongly averse to war. He married Anne of Denmark; their eldest son Henry, Prince of Wales, was a popular and charming youth, greatly mourned when he died in 1612. During this reign Shakespeare, Jonson, and Bacon flourished and the new translation of the Bible – the King James Version – was published. In James's later years it is possible that homosexual tendencies emerged: he had several favourites, of whom George Villiers, created Duke of Buckingham, was the best known.

94. James I by Daniel Mytens, 1621. 58½ × 39½ in (148.5 × 100 cm). National Portrait Gallery

Charles I

b. 1600; r. **1625-49**

The second son of James I, Charles was lonely and rather frail as a boy. As a king he was a generous patron of the arts. His obstinacy and absolutism as a ruler led eventually to civil war and to his downfall. In 1629, after a quarrel with Parliament over the impeachment of Buckingham, he dissolved it – it did not meet for the next eleven years – and imposed the taxes that it had refused to sanction. Unrest mounted over his application of the principle of divine right and his enforcement of Anglican forms of worship which excluded Calvinists and Presbyterians. In Scotland opposition came from those who vowed fidelity to the Presbyterian Kirk, the 'Coven-

anters'. To make matters worse Charles's wife, to whom he was devoted, was Henrietta Maria, daughter of Henri IV of France, and his Protestant subjects were suspicious of a Catholic queen. In 1642 civil war between the Roundheads (Parliamentarians) and Cavaliers (Royalists) erupted over Parliament's demand to approve the king's choice of ministers. Charles was tried for treason to the realm and died on the scaffold in 1649.

95. *Above:* the image of Charles I was fashioned for posterity, in a series of portraits showing many facets of his role as king, by Van Dyck. The famous 'three-in-one' was painted about 1637 as a model from which Bernini in Rome could carve a bust. Oil on canvas, 33 × 39 in (84 × 99 cm). Royal Collection

97. *Right:* the final tragic stage in one of the richest of royal iconographies is Edward Bower's record of Charles I at his trial, 1648 (detail). Oil, $51\frac{1}{2}$ × 39 in (131 × 99 cm). H.M. The Queen Mother

Elizabeth of Bohemia

1596-1662

Known as the 'Winter Queen', she was the daughter of James I, sister of Charles I and Prince Henry to whom she was particularly close. She was pretty and much loved. In 1613 she married Frederick V, the Elector Palatine, whom the Bohemians elected as king; he ruled for under one year before being forced to flee from the Catholic Imperial army at the start of the Thirty Years' War. Elizabeth lived in straitened circumstances throughout most of her life, returning to England shortly before her death in 1662. She had thirteen children, including Sophia, the mother of George I, and Prince Rupert of the Rhine, who fought valiantly for his uncle Charles I in the Civil War.

96. *Right:* Elizabeth of Bohemia, by the studio of Gerrit Honthorst. 1642. Panel, 26 × 21½ in (66 × 55 cm). National Portrait Gallery

98. *Below right:* Henrietta Maria, wife of Charles I, with her dwarf, by Van Dyck. 1633. Canvas, 86 × 53 in (219 × 135 cm). National Gallery of Art, Washington DC – Samuel H. Kress Coll.

99. Charles the Martyr, engraving of Charles I by William Marshall. British Museum

The Explanation of the EMBLEME.

Ponderibus *genus omne mali, probriq̃ gravatus,*
Vixeq̃ *ferenda ferens,* Palma ut Depressa, *resurgo.*

Though clogg'd with weights of miseries
Palm-like Depress'd, I higher rise.

Ac, *velut undarum* Fluctûs Ventiq̃, *furorem*
Irati Populi Rupes immota *repello.*
Clarior è tenebris, *cœlestis stella, corusco.*
(Victor et æternùm—felici *pace* triumpho.

And as th'unmoved Rock out-brave's
The boistrous Windes and rageing waves:
So triumph I. And shine more bright
In sad Affliction's Darksom night.

Auro Fulgentem *rutilo gemmisq̃ micantem,*
At curis Gravidam *spernendo* calco Coronam.

That Splendid, but yet toilsom Crown
Regardlesly I trample down.

Spinosam, *at ferri facilem, quo* Spes mea, Christi
Auxilio, Nobis *non est* tractare *molestum.*

With joie I take this Crown of thorn,
Though sharp, yet easie to be born.

Æternam, *fixis fidei, semperq̃—*beatam
In Cœlos *oculis* Specto, Nobisq̃ *paratam.*

That heav'nlie Crown, already mine,
I View with eies of Faith divine.

Quod Vanum *est, sperno; quod* Christi Gratia *præbet*
Amplecti *studium est:* Virtutis Gloria *merces.*

I slight vain things; and do embrace
Glorie, the just reward of Grace.

Oliver Cromwell

1599-1658

Victorious leader of the Parliamentarians, Cromwell led the Commonwealth for nine years from 1649 to his death in 1658; during the last three years of his life he was Lord Protector. A country squire by background, he was a stern patriot governed by commonsense and piety of a rough and unyielding order. He was a brave soldier and fought many battles against both Charles I and Charles II, but he was a repressive leader and was disliked for his unbending Puritan rule.

100. As head of state, Cromwell had to be portrayed formally, and in the last representation of all, his funeral effigy, he appears as a monarch, crowned and robed. Engraving (detail), British Museum

101. Oliver Cromwell's famous comment to a portrait painter that he paint him 'warts and all' is best illustrated in this unfinished miniature by Samuel Cooper. Duke of Buccleuch Coll.

Charles II

b. 1630; r. **1660-85**

At the Restoration of 1660 Charles II was brought back from France, where he had fled in 1645. He had returned to be crowned in Scotland in 1651, but after the execution of his most trusted supporter, Montrose, he had been once again forced to flee, making a series of legendary escapes. After his long years of exile he was determined never to go 'on his travels' again, and by astute management kept the throne until his death. He combined a light touch and a love of pleasure with a sound grasp of politics. Witty, cynical but charming, he was known as the 'Merry Monarch' and had many mistresses, chief among them Barbara, Lady Castlemaine, Louise de Kerouaille, Duchess of Portsmouth, and the orange-seller Nell Gwynne. He married the Portuguese princess Catherine of Braganza, but had no legitimate children; he did, however, have a large number of illegitimate sons by his mistresses, and they founded several ducal houses. His reign saw the Great Plague (1665) and the Great Fire of London (1666). The arts and sciences flourished under him with such outstanding men as Pepys, Wren, Dryden and Newton.

102. *Above:* Charles II, bust by Honoré Pellé, 1684. Height 51 in (130 cm). Victoria and Albert Museum

103. *Left:* Catherine of Braganza, unfinished miniature by Samuel Cooper. 5×4 in (13× 10 cm). Royal Collection

104. Charles II, attributed to Thomas Hawker. Sir Peter Lely was Charles's court painter, but he sat to many other artists. This formal portrait shows him in old age, with a compelling, not unattractive, ugliness in the midst of his wig and robes. Canvas, $89 \times 53\frac{1}{2}$ in (226×136 cm). National Portrait Gallery

James II

b. 1633; r. **1685-88**

Younger son of Charles I, James was an avowed Catholic. As Duke of York, he had been an unpopular choice as successor, but by the time his brother Charles II died he was accepted. He first married Anne Hyde, who died before he came to the throne; their two daughters, Mary and Anne, were brought up as Protestants. In 1673 he married the Italian princess Mary of Modena, a Catholic. James's liberal approach to freedom of worship for Catholics provoked rebellion, notably by the Duke of Monmouth, his illegitimate nephew, who was executed with his followers by Judge Jeffreys. When it appeared that James might reinstate Catholicism by force, and when his heir James Edward was born in 1688, seven of the most notable Anglican bishops and lords sought help from William of Orange, his son-in-law and the nearest Protestant male relative. James fled to Ireland, but he was by now demoralized and was decisively defeated by William at the Battle of the Boyne in 1690. He died eleven years later, an exile in France.

105. James II as Duke of York with his first wife, Anne Hyde, by Sir Peter Lely. 1660s. 55 × 75 in (140 × 192 cm). National Portrait Gallery

106. James II as Duke
of York, miniature by
Samuel Cooper. 1661.
Victoria and Albert
Museum

107. James Edward
Stuart, miniature after
A.S. Belle. National
Portrait Gallery

James Edward Stuart (The Old Pretender)

1688-1766

The Catholic son of James II and Mary of
Modena, he was excluded from the succession
by the Act of Settlement of 1701. He was,
however, recognized as King by the French
and Spanish, but was never allowed back to
England and was given asylum in France.
Discontent in Scotland and elsewhere helped
foment rebellion on his behalf in 1715. In his
youth he was courageous on the battlefield,
but he was a dull fellow, and later his fortunes
declined and he was quickly forgotten. He
married Clementina Sobieska of Poland,
granddaughter of the great King John
Sobieski.

109. *Above:* William III was a reluctant sitter; Kneller produced the standard state portrait in quantity, but the battle pieces are much livelier, as this one by Jan Wyck, 1696. Detail. Collection Lord Egremont, Petworth

108. *Left:* in James II's brief tenure of the throne, Sir Godfrey Kneller was his main painter. This painting by Kneller originated before his accession, showing him as Lord High Admiral: the design was then altered, a crown inserted and his admiral's baton changed into a sceptre. 1684–5. Canvas, 93 × 57 in (236 × 145 cm). National Portrait Gallery

110. Prince Charles Edward Stuart, attributed to H.D. Hamilton. c. 1785. 10 × 9 in (25 × 23 cm). National Portrait Gallery

Charles Edward Stuart (The Young Pretender)

1720-88

Charles was born in Rome in 1720; he was handsome and attractive, capable of inspiring great devotion among his followers. From early on he turned his attention to claiming his 'rightful' throne, and trained himself rigorously to that end. In 1745 he landed at Moidart on the west coast of Scotland and raised his standard at Glenfinnan. He marched on to Edinburgh where he declared his father King and won the battle of Prestonpans. With the support of the Highlanders he advanced south, but found the English apathetic to his cause. In 1746 he was pursued back to Culloden, where the Scots suffered a terrible slaughter at the hands of the Duke of Cumberland, son of George II. Charles was rescued by loyal Highlanders like Flora Macdonald, and fled to France. From there he went on to Rome where he sustained an increasingly drunken existence and died in 1788.

William III

b. 1650; r. **1688-1702**

Mary II

b. 1662; r. **1688-94**

Son of William II of Orange and Mary, sister of Charles II and James II, William married his cousin Mary, the elder daughter of James II. They were joint rulers from the Glorious Revolution of 1688, when he was summoned to re-establish Protestantism, until her death of smallpox; thereafter he ruled alone. His prime concern on the Continent was the war with Louis XIV; in Ireland, 'King Billy' won the Battle of the Boyne, a Protestant victory still vividly remembered there. Although rather cold as a personality, his courage and determination in securing victory over Louis XIV and his political acumen in developing an effective constitutional settlement make William III one of the greatest kings Britain has had. Mary was kindly, virtuous and dutiful, but their marriage was childless and joyless. She was the patron of Purcell, who wrote several birthday odes for her and composed her moving funeral march.

Anne

b. 1665; r. **1702-14**

Anne was James II's younger daughter and the last Stuart monarch. She married Prince George of Denmark. It was a happy marriage, marred by failure to produce a healthy child – she had at least ten miscarriages and five children, all of whom died young. The only one to survive for any length of time, William, succumbed at the age of eleven. She was quiet and led a somewhat dull life; she herself inspired no great emotion, but her mighty soldier John Churchill (later Duke of Marlborough) and his wife Sarah, the Queen's dearest friend, provided a touch of brilliance. His victories over the French included the Battle of Blenheim in 1704, after which he named the magnificent house Vanbrugh built for him in Oxfordshire. In Anne's reign the English and Scottish nations were merged by the Act of Union (1702). Among the great men of her age were Addison, Swift and Vanbrugh.

112. William III by G. Schalcken. $29\frac{1}{2} \times 24\frac{1}{2}$ in (75×62 cm). Attingham Park, National Trust

111. *Left:* Mary II by Jan van der Vaart. Detail. Audley End

113. *Above:* Wigless
head of William III's
wax effigy, in
Westminster Abbey

114. Queen Anne,
attributed to M. Dahl,
c. 1690. 92 × 56 in
(234 × 142 cm).
National Portrait
Gallery

THE HOUSE OF HANOVER

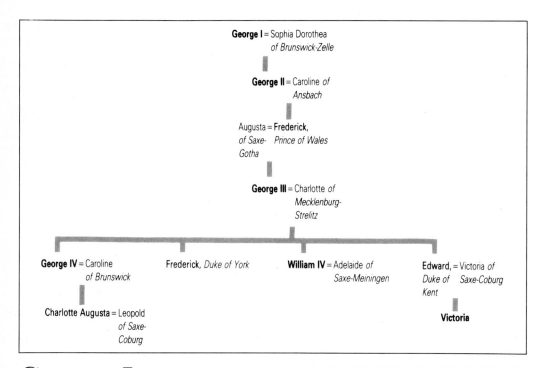

George I = Sophia Dorothea
of Brunswick-Zelle

George II = Caroline of
Ansbach

Augusta = Frederick,
of Saxe-   Prince of Wales
Gotha

George III = Charlotte of
Mecklenburg-
Strelitz

George IV = Caroline   Frederick, Duke of York   William IV = Adelaide of   Edward, = Victoria of
of Brunswick   Saxe-Meiningen   Duke of   Saxe-Coburg
                                                                                  Kent

Charlotte Augusta = Leopold   Victoria
of Saxe-
Coburg

George I

b. 1660; r. **1714-27**

When Queen Anne died the nearest Protestant
blood-relative of the Stuarts was George,
Elector of Hanover. He was the grandson of
Elizabeth of Bohemia, the Winter Queen,
through his mother Sophia who married
Ernest Augustus, Elector of Hanover. At the
date of his accession he was already fifty-three,
had been Elector for some years and had no
interest in England. For thirty years he had
kept his wife, Sophia, a state prisoner in his
Hanoverian capital because of her adultery;
she never came to England but many of his
mistresses did. Although he was fussy, obstinate and wanted the government to do his
bidding, his inability to communicate in
English – he is said to have talked to his
ministers in dog-Latin – meant that he left the
affairs of state to be manipulated by a handful
of Whig leaders who effectively ruled in his
name. He was always on bad terms with his
son, afterwards George II.

George II

b. 1683; r. **1727-60**

According to his chief minister Robert Walpole, George II was the 'greatest political

115. *Left:* George I
was the fifth monarch
in succession to have
his (fairly uninspired)
state portrait
manufactured by Sir
Godfrey Kneller (the
king was an
unenthusiastic sitter).
Kneller's profile here –
a study for the coinage
– is both livelier and
more truly regal.
c. 1714. Canvas, 30 ×
25 in (76 × 63.5 cm).
National Portrait
Gallery.

116. *Right:* The most
vivid painted image of
George II is by J.M.
Pyne, showing the
king in old age. 1759.
Audley End

117. George II's portraiture has been described as 'a confusing and depressing' subject. Although he was painted as an equestrian commander, the best heroic image is in sculpture, the laureate bust by J.M. Rysbrack, 1738. Terracotta. Royal Collection

coward who ever wore the crown'. He made himself popular by leading his troops in battle at Dettingen in 1743 – the last British king who actually fought. He also had to deal with the 1745 rebellion led by the Young Pretender. He married Caroline of Ansbach who developed with Walpole, the first real Prime Minister, a close personal and working friendship. She was a great patron of the arts, especially of Handel; at the first performance of his *Messiah* the King rose to his feet for the Hallelujah chorus, and this gesture has been followed by British audiences ever since. He was also, however, notorious, perhaps rather unjustly, as the Teutonic monarch who hated 'boetry and bainting'. He continued his father's policy of governmental restraint and relied on his wife, the great Whig families and his ministers to run the country. He also continued to rule Hanover, combining in his European campaigns the interests of the two nations.

118. Queen Caroline, wife of George II, bust by J.M. Rysbrack. Terracotta. Royal Collection

Frederick, Prince of Wales

119. Frederick, Prince of Wales, by P. Mercier, c. 1736–8. (Present whereabouts unknown)

1707-51

Nicknamed 'Fritz' by his father who disliked him, Frederick, after a serious quarrel between them in 1736, set up a 'rival court', where he patronized the arts and provided a focus for the opposition to Walpole. He married Augusta of Saxe-Gotha. When told of his death, George II, who was at a game of cards, did not interrupt the game but calmly announced to the company, 'Fritz is dead.'

George III

b. 1738; r. **1760-1820**

George succeeded his grandfather at the age of twenty-two. He was a man of simple tastes, conscientious and industrious, devoted to his wife, Charlotte of Mecklenburg-Strelitz; he was popular with his subjects to whom he was known affectionately as 'Farmer George'. His reign saw two great national revolutions, each of which had most far-reaching consequences for the world. His government's unyielding stance on the granting of rights to the American colonies led to the Declaration of Independence by them in 1776, and the war which followed lost Britain the colonies, although Canada remained loyal to the crown. In 1789 the French Revolution began; the war which followed against Napoleon was conducted by the younger Pitt with the help of Nelson's and, later, Wellington's heroic exploits. After the famous occasion in 1787 on which the king was seen to address an oak tree, his intermittent bouts of instability caused by hereditary porphyria became more frequent, and in 1811 Parliament appointed the Prince of Wales Regent.

120. *Above:* Queen Charlotte at her dressing-table, by Johann Zoffany. 1766-7. Oil on canvas, 44 × 51 in (112 × 129.5 cm). Windsor, Royal Collection

121. *Right:* The little painting of George III by P.E. Stroehling catches something of his relatively modest, domesticated side at Windsor. 1807. Detail. Oil on copper, 24 × 19 in (61 × 48 cm). Royal Collection

122. *Above:* M.C. Wyatt's delightful statue of George III is one of the few modest equestrian statues. Cockspur Street, London

123. *Below:* George III's first state portrait, almost mass-produced by Allan Ramsay's studio, was one of the most successful. Later he was painted by Gainsborough, Reynolds, Beechey, Lawrence and others. c. 1767. Canvas, 58 × 42 in (147 × 107 cm). National Portrait Gallery

George IV

b. 1762; r. **1820-30**

The regency of 'Prinny', as the future king was known, encouraged a brilliant period of fashionable licence and gaiety. A sensitive and active patron of the arts, he was responsible to a great extent for the architectural splendours of the Brighton Pavilion, Regent Street and the Nash terraces round Regent's Park. In 1785 he married Maria Fitzherbert, a Catholic widow – a marriage Parliament declared illegal. Ten years later he was forced to marry Caroline of Brunswick, an unattractive and uncouth personality; they separated shortly afterwards in mutual dislike. On his accession she returned to England expecting to be crowned queen, but instead was put on trial for adultery. The English people savoured the spectacle of this public quarrel:

'Most gracious queen, we thee implore
To go away and sin no more;
But if that effort be too great,
To go away, at any rate'.

During George's regency and reign Napoleon was defeated and England began to recover from the long period of war, although his excesses and self-indulgence made his impoverished people resentful, and he was bitterly satirized by the leading newspapers and cartoonists of the day.

124. *Above:* a more mundane, portly (and new-fangledly trousered) view than in the Lawrence portrait (plate 14) is given by the silhouette of George IV with his brother the Duke of York. 12 × 9 in (30.5 × 23 cm). National Portrait Gallery

125, 126. George IV, silver crown piece, 1826. British Museum

127. George IV as Prince of Wales, on horseback,
by George Stubbs (detail). Oil on canvas, 40½ × 50 in
(102.5 × 127.5 cm). Royal Collection

128. Caroline of Brunswick, wife of George IV, by S. Lane. 36 × 28 in (91 × 70.5 cm). Scottish National Portrait Gallery

129. Charlotte Augusta, Princess of Wales, by G. Dawe. Canvas, 55 × 42½ in (140 × 108 cm). National Portrait Gallery

Charlotte Augusta

1796-1817

The only child of the brief and disastrous union between George IV and Caroline, Charlotte Princess of Wales was born in 1796. Despite a lonely and unhappy childhood in which she had little contact with her parents and was brought up by governesses, she had unquenchable high spirits and a strong sense of independence. Described as wholesomely pretty, she chose her own husband, Leopold of Saxe-Coburg. Both she and her child died in childbirth when she was twenty. If the child had lived it would have inherited the throne.

William IV

b. 1765; r. **1830-37**

William was the younger brother of George IV and third son of George III. He was known as the 'Sailor King' and was bluff, fairly popular and mildly eccentric. He was known for his garrulity and behaved foolishly from time to time, but was nevertheless a kindly man. With a long naval service behind him, his first interest was the navy and the sea – he had been friends with Nelson. In 1818 he married Adelaide of Saxe-Meiningen; their two children both died in infancy. Previously he had lived with the actress Mrs Jordan who bore him ten children. He encouraged his ministers to push through the 1832 Parliamentary Reform Bill, thereby displaying a somewhat unexpected streak of wisdom.

130. William IV. Relatively few portraits were made in his short reign. This watercolour is by an unknown artist. 10½ × 8½ in (26.5 × 21.5 cm). National Portrait Gallery

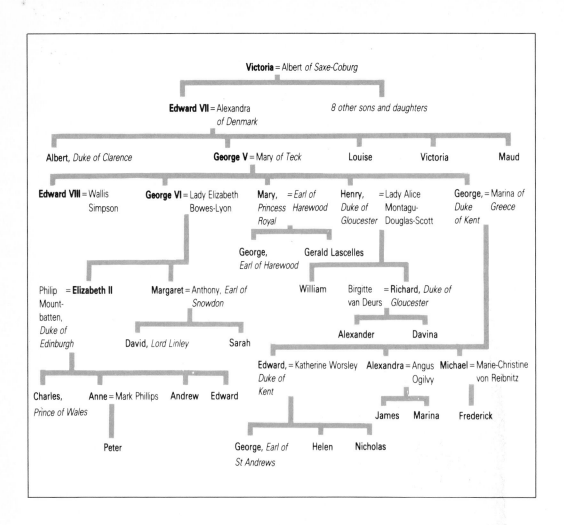

Victoria = Albert *of Saxe-Coburg*

Edward VII = Alexandra *of Denmark*   ·   *8 other sons and daughters*

Albert, *Duke of Clarence*   ·   **George V** = Mary *of Teck*   ·   Louise   ·   Victoria   ·   Maud

Edward VIII = Wallis Simpson   ·   **George VI** = Lady Elizabeth Bowes-Lyon   ·   Mary, *Princess Royal* = *Earl of* Harewood   ·   Henry, *Duke of Gloucester* = Lady Alice Montagu-Douglas-Scott   ·   George, *Duke of Kent* = Marina *of Greece*

George, *Earl of Harewood*   ·   Gerald Lascelles

Philip Mountbatten, *Duke of Edinburgh* = **Elizabeth II**   ·   Margaret = Anthony, *Earl of Snowdon*

William   ·   Birgitte van Deurs = Richard, *Duke of Gloucester*

David, *Lord Linley*   ·   Sarah

Alexander   ·   Davina

Edward, *Duke of Kent* = Katherine Worsley   ·   Alexandra = Angus Ogilvy   ·   Michael = Marie-Christine von Reibnitz

Charles, *Prince of Wales*   ·   Anne = Mark Phillips   ·   Andrew   ·   Edward

James   ·   Marina   ·   Frederick

Peter

George, *Earl of St Andrews*   ·   Helen   ·   Nicholas

131. *Far left:* The official painter of Victoria's early career as queen was the German court painter F.X. Winterhalter. Watercolour (detail), 1855. Windsor, Royal Collection

132. *Left:* Victoria was the first monarch to be subject to the camera, and early photographs contrast strongly with the Winterhalter, such as this one by J. Mayall, 1855. Windsor Castle Library, Royal Collection

THE HOUSES OF SAXE-COBURG AND WINDSOR

Victoria

b. 1819; r. **1837-1901**

Daughter of Edward, Duke of Kent, George III's fourth son, and Victoria of Saxe-Coburg, Victoria came to the throne at eighteen. In 1841 she married her cousin Prince Albert of Saxe-Coburg. She was a devoted wife and had nine children, among whose descendants were most of the kings and queens of Europe, including the last Kaiser, Wilhelm II. Albert had a keen interest in the arts and sciences; he instigated the Great Exhibition of 1851 designed for the expansion of industrialization. He was a great influence on, and help to,

Victoria. After his death in 1861 of typhoid she was heartbroken and withdrew from the public gaze for many years. She emerged to be created Empress of India in 1877. She presided over the glory of the British Empire and the establishment of Britain as a powerful and peaceful industrialized nation. She exerted an immense influence, stamping the era with her own rather stiff respectability, tastes and morals, referred to as 'Balmorality' after she took to staying in her Scottish castle designed by Albert. Of her two most famous ministers, Victoria disliked Gladstone, but adored Disraeli. By the end of her reign she was a revered old lady, having won the attachment of her subjects. She lived to celebrate both her gold and diamond jubilees.

133. Edward, Duke of Kent and Strathearn, father of Queen Victoria, by W. Beechey, 1818 (detail). Canvas, 29 × 24 in (73.5 × 61 cm). National Portrait Gallery

134. The most convincing and humane image of Victoria later in life is Sir William Nicholson's woodcut of 1900. From a series of twelve portraits for the *New Review*

135. *Left:* the painting of Queen Victoria by Thomas Sully catches something of the charm of her youth. Wallace Collection

136. *Right:* the camera was the first medium to catch a royal smile of Victoria, contrary to tradition, amused. By Charles Knight, taken 15 February 1898. Windsor Castle Library, Royal Collection

137. *Above:* another novel mode of image-making was in postage-stamps, such as the penny black. Here the profile of Victoria is based on a drawing by Henry Corbould, in turn based on a medal of 1838 by William Wyon

138. *Right: Four Generations*, by W. Orchardson (Queen Victoria, Edward VII, George V, the Duke of Windsor). Oil on canvas, 21 × 28 in (53 × 71 cm). National Portrait Gallery

Edward VII

b. 1841; r. **1901-10**

Aged fifty-nine at his accession, Edward was a popular king whose outlook and morals as displayed when he was Prince of Wales were in sharp contrast to those of his mother. The gay days of the naughty Nineties were led and characterized by him. In 1863 he married Alexandra of Denmark, who survived him by 15 years. Since his mother refused him any role in government because she considered him unreliable, he turned to the pleasures of travel, horses and women. He had many mistresses, the most famous being Daisy, Countess of Warwick, Lillie Langtry and Alice Keppel. His charm was a factor in persuading France to accept the Entente Cordiale in 1904. He gave his name to the Edwardian age, a period which was colourful, opulent and somewhat vulgar, the 'last summer' before the irrevocable change wrought in Europe by world war and the consequences for modern society.

George V

b. 1865; r. **1910-36**

His elder brother, the Duke of Clarence, having died in 1892 (in circumstances touched with a breath of scandal, never satisfactorily explained), George Duke of York, succeeded his father Edward VII. He married his brother's fiancée May (Mary) of Teck in 1893; she died in 1953. He enjoyed a happy family life and was a solid and dutiful king. He established the concept of the Royal Family as a model for his subjects; he was also the first to broadcast the Christmas message to the people, which is now as much a part of Christmas as the other traditions. His was the modern style of monarchy, acting only on the advice of his ministers. By threatening, on Asquith's advice, to create new peers to swamp opposition to the Parliamentary Reform Bill in 1911, George V obliged the House of Lords to vote for the limitation of its own powers. His reign also saw the development of the Labour movement and of its first government. As Emperor of India he visited that country for the Durbar or convocation of Delhi in 1911.

141. *Above:* Queen Alexandra — then Princess of Wales — as Doctor of Music, statue by Count von Gleichen, 1891. Royal College of Music

139. *Above left:* Edward VII in his first motor-car, April 1902. Windsor Castle Library, Royal Collection

140. *Left:* George V making his first Christmas Broadcast in 1934. Windsor Castle Library, Royal Collection

142. *Right:* Edward VII, replica of the state portrait, by Sir Luke Fildes. 108½ × 71 in (276 × 180 cm). National Portrait Gallery

144. *Below:* Queen Mary, by Sir Oswald Birley (detail). 1934. 45 × 38 in (114 × 96.5 cm). Royal Collection

145. *Above right:* Edward VIII by Walter Sickert. Painted from a newspaper photograph, 1936. 72 × 36 in (183 × 91 cm). Beaverbrook Art Gallery, Fredericton, New Brunswick, Canada

146. *Right:* Edward VIII, 1½d stamp, 1936. The stamp portrait promised well, a welcome echo of the simplicity and dignity of Victoria's first stamps

143. *Left:* this life-scale portrait by Sir John Lavery of George V with Queen Mary and their children is a very formal version of the traditional family 'conversation piece'. 1913. 134 × 107 in (340 × 272 cm). National Portrait Gallery, on loan from H.I. Spottiswoode

Edward VIII

b. 1894; r. **1936**; d. 1972

As Prince of Wales, Edward – called David by his family – was popular, a leader of fashion and a charmer of hearts; he also worked hard to understand the problems of the people. He reigned for only a few months before abdicating to marry Mrs Wallis Simpson, a twice-divorced American with whom he had fallen in love. In a moving message broadcast to his subjects throughout the world he explained that he could not contemplate ruling 'without the help and support of the woman I love'. His decision seemed to some a romantic necessity, to others a grave evasion of duty. What kind of king he would have made is unclear. He was known to have admired some aspects of Hitler. He was given the title of Duke of Windsor and went into exile; he died in 1972. The Duchess lives in Paris; there were no children.

George VI

b. 1895; r. 1936-52

Edward VIII's younger brother, having been brought up without any expectation of succeeding to the throne, the Duke of York – Bertie, as he was known – was unprepared for the shock of becoming king. He was always shy and for many years suffered from a stammer. A strong sense of duty, however, led him to conquer his nervousness and fear of public occasions. He married Lady Elizabeth Bowes-Lyon in 1923; he was much respected for his exemplary family life. In the First World War he saw service in the Navy and later was the first member of the Royal Family to become a qualified pilot. He inspired devotion when he and the Queen stayed in London during the Second World War, showing great courage. His widow, the Queen Mother, is today held in the highest public esteem and affection.

148. *Above:* bronze bust of George VI by W.R. Dick. Height 15 in (38 cm). National Portrait Gallery

147. *Left:* George VI by R.G. Eves (detail). 40 × 20 in (102 × 51 cm). National Portrait Gallery

149. *Right:* King George VI, state portrait by Sir Gerald Kelly. 107 × 68 in (272 × 173 cm). Royal Collection

151. *Above:* the Queen is the first monarch to be subjected to the almost ceaseless scrutiny of press and television cameras whenever she appears in public. This is the moment of crowning during the Coronation Service in Westminster Abbey, 1953

H.M. Queen Elizabeth II

150. *Left:* this small-scale portrait by Sir James Gunn of George VI with Queen Elizabeth (now the Queen Mother), the Princesses Elizabeth (now Queen Elizabeth II) and Margaret is an immensely popular picture – the reflection of a relaxed attitude to the monarchy. 1950. 59½ × 39½ in (151 × 100 cm). National Portrait Gallery

b. 1926; r. **from 1952**

Born in 1926, Elizabeth came to the throne on the death of her father in February 1952. Since her coronation in 1953 she has become the most photographed, written about and, in a sense, hounded monarch in the world. The monarchy now has little executive power, but her power of example is widely felt. She has inspired love and respect not only for her devotion to her family, but for her scrupulous attention to duty. By her frequent foreign tours she has displayed her willingness to help preserve the family of nations of the Commonwealth and the cause of peace between nations. She married Prince Philip Mountbatten of Greece in 1947; her four children are, Charles, Prince of Wales, born 1948, now married to Lady Diana Spencer and with one child, Prince William, born 1982; Anne, born 1950, now married to Mark Phillips, and with two children, Peter and Zara; Andrew, born 1960 and Edward, born 1964.

152. *Left:* the Queen studying the form of some of her racehorses on the Berkshire Downs, with her trainer. A still from the film *Royal Family*

155. *Right:* Prince Charles in naval uniform, October 1978

H.R.H. The Prince of Wales

b. 1948

153. *Far left:* the Queen on 'walkabout' at RAF Honington, Suffolk, June 1979

154. *Left:* the Duke of Edinburgh hands over his Queen's Flight helicopter to its RAF pilot and to the cameraman and director of the *Royal Family* film, Peter Bartlett and Richard Cawston

156. *Right:* Prince Charles at Balmoral on his thirtieth birthday, November 1978. He wears the Hunting Stewart tartan

Prince Charles was invested with the title of Prince of Wales in 1969. An energetic young man, he pursues a wide spectrum of interests ranging from polo to opera. After leaving Cambridge, he spent some years in the Navy, is a qualified pilot, and is now vigorously addressing himself to the rigours of representing Britain in visits abroad and promoting her interests, as well as heading charities and being patron of countless societies and institutions. He is unlikely to be king for some time, but will probably not suffer from the same frustrations as Edward VII in a similar situation. He is extremely popular, and his marriage to Lady Diana Spencer on 29 July 1981 was watched on television throughout the world.

157. *Left:* the Prince and Princess of Wales on their Wedding Day, 29 July 1981, are shown here with the Queen and other members of the Royal Family and the bride's parents, Earl and Countess Spencer. By permission of Colour Library International.

158. *Right:* the official state portrait of Queen Elizabeth II was by Sir James Gunn, but Pietro Annigoni's first portrait of her was much more popular, and copies of it have very often served as official portraits. 1955. Oil on canvas, 59 × 39 in (150 × 99 cm). Fishmongers' Hall, London

Acknowledgements

The publishers and John Calmann & Cooper Ltd wish to thank the museums, galleries and other institutions and the private collectors who have kindly given permission for their works to be reproduced. Those owners not listed below are acknowledged in the captions.

The works in the Royal Collection (frontispiece, nos. 6, 18, 21, 63, 66, 68, 75, 89, 91, 93, 95, 103, 117, 118, 120, 121, 127, 131, 132, 136, 139, 140, 144, 149) are reproduced by gracious permission of Her Majesty The Queen; no. 97 by gracious permission of Her Majesty The Queen Mother.

Nos. 33, 34, 49, 52, 54, 56, 58, 71, 113 are reproduced by courtesy of the Dean and Chapter of Westminster Abbey; no. 48 by courtesy of the Dean and Chapter of Worcester Cathedral; no. 53 by courtesy of the Dean and Chapter of Gloucester Cathedral; no. 64 by courtesy of the Archbishop of Canterbury and the Trustees of Lambeth Palace Library.

Nos. 73 and 74 are Crown copyright; nos. 11 and 111 are reproduced with the permission of the Controller of HMSO.

No. 116 is reproduced by kind permission of the Hon. R. H. C. Neville; no. 143 by kind permission of Mr H. I. Spottiswoode, Littlehampton; nos. 137 and 146 with the permission of the Post Office.

Thanks are also due to the following photographers, firms and institutions who kindly supplied photographs: Archives Photographiques, Paris; the British Museum; A. C. Cooper Ltd; the Courtauld Institute; ITC Ltd; A. F. Kersting; the Mansell Collection; the National Portrait Gallery; Phaidon Press Ltd; Photo Giraudon; Photo Marburg; Photo Studios Ltd; the Press Association; the Radio Times Hulton Picture Library; the Royal Academy of Arts; the Warburg Institute.

Bibliography

Eric Linklater, *The Royal House of Scotland*, Macmillan 1970

Christopher Brooke, *The Saxon and Norman Kings*, Batsford 1963

W. L. Warren, *King John*, Eyre & Spottiswoode 1961

Paul M. Kendall, *Warwick the Kingmaker*, Allen & Unwin 1957

Morris Bishop, *The Penguin Book of the Middle Ages*, 1971

G. M. Trevelyan, *A Shortened History of England*, 1959

The Pelican History of England: *The Seventeenth Century*, Maurice Ashley, 1952
The Eighteenth Century, J. H. Plumb, 1950
The Nineteenth Century, David Thomson, 1950

A Dictionary of Modern History 1789-1945, Cresset 1962

The Dictionary of National Biography